REAPING THE BENEFITS OF INDUSTRY 4.0 THROUGH SKILLS DEVELOPMENT IN VIET NAM

JANUARY 2021

ASIAN DEVELOPMENT BANK

ADB

Contents

Tables, Figures, and Boxes

iv

Foreword

Talent and skills are valuable in powering knowledge-based economies. The Fourth Industrial Revolution (4IR) has ushered in extraordinary technological advances, fusing boundaries of physical, digital, and biological worlds to create new paradigms in the way we live, work, and interact. These trends have heralded excitement and fear—excitement in advancing frontiers of human endeavor and fear of negative repercussions on jobs and rising inequalities.

To respond to questions and concerns in developing member countries of the Asian Development Bank (ADB) on how their economies can transition effectively to 4IR, the study *"Reaping the Benefits of Industry 4.0 Through Skills Development in High-Growth Industries in Southeast Asia"* builds an evidence based on opportunities, challenges, and promising approaches in 4IR. It covers Cambodia, Indonesia, the Philippines, and Viet Nam with specific focus on two industries in each country deemed important for growth, employment, and 4IR: tourism and garments in Cambodia, food and beverage manufacturing and automotive manufacturing in Indonesia, information technology and business process outsourcing and electronics in the Philippines, and agro-processing and logistics in Viet Nam.

Much has been written about anticipated loss of millions of jobs arising from automation. At ADB, we take a tempered view. The study reaffirms a positive outlook to 4IR creating new opportunities for quality jobs. While many jobs will indeed be lost as a result of automation, new jobs will emerge through the adoption of technologies that will increase worker productivity and competitiveness of nations, thereby leading to greater prosperity. However, tapping such benefits is predicated on increasing investments in skills development and greater efforts by companies to upskill their workforce to perform new and higher order roles in complementarity with machines.

Adoption of 4IR technologies can increase efficiency and productivity. They enable real-time tracking of supply chains for production and inventory management of raw materials and finished goods. Use of artificial intelligence and machine learning can provide insights into consumer behavior to customize production. Robotic process automation can relieve tedious and repetitive labor-intensive activities, allowing time for higher order functions. Augmented reality and virtual reality can be helpful to train workers in new tasks that they were not familiar with, or skilled in, earlier. Application of 4IR technologies helps developing countries move up the value chain in their products and services. Timely skills development can ensure that automation and artificial intelligence can benefit workers at large.

The study has resulted in a suite of country reports for Cambodia, Indonesia, the Philippines, and Viet Nam, and a synthesis report that captures common elements across the four. They seek to provide policy makers with research and evidence-based solutions for skills and talent development to strengthen the countries' readiness for a transition to 4IR.

The role of governments is crucial in ensuring equitable access to skills development. We expect to see a new balance between physical and virtual workplaces as the gig economy, where employers increasingly rely on part-time freelance workers on short-term contracts, takes firmer position, and widespread digital transformation of citizen services that call for basic digital capabilities in all population groups and rising opportunities for those with advanced digital skills. Job losses will be real, however, a well-prepared 4IR strategy with industry transformation roadmaps that are recommended in the study can convert disruptions to opportunities to pivot the workforce to new and modern occupations.

The study was completed prior to the coronavirus disease (COVID-19). It is apparent that COVID-19 is accelerating digital transformation. Companies deploying 4IR technologies are likely to recover faster from heavy disruptions arising from the pandemic and be more resilient in the future. Beyond COVID-19, market analysts predict a 'new normal' where digital strategies adopted during the lockdown due to the pandemic will pick up pace. Consumer and producer behavior will most likely be altered permanently with greater digital exposure. The study's recommendations to strengthen widespread digital capabilities, enhance online/distance learning, digital platforms, education technology (EdTech), and simulation-based learning have become more relevant in the aftermath of COVID-19. The study also points to the scope for closer collaboration between public and private sectors, which is also quite relevant in the COVID-19 context. The findings of this study are thus very timely in the discourse to facilitate a sustainable bounce-back from COVID-19, as countries aspire for accelerating economic diversification and boosting competitiveness using the pandemic as an opportunity for structural reforms.

We welcome your feedback on this report and continued engagement with all stakeholders.

Woochong Um
Director General
Sustainable Development and
Climate Change Department

Ramesh Subramaniam
Director General
South East Asia Department

Preface and Acknowledgments

The ADB study *Reaping the Benefits of Industry 4.0 Through Skills Development in High-Growth Industries in Southeast Asia* marks our effort to bridge research, policy, and practice on the implications of the Fourth Industrial Revolution (4IR) on future job markets. To effectively address this forward-looking topic, the study made use of various sources of secondary information and sought to triangulate information from different primary sources. It included a survey of employers, a survey of training institutions on their readiness for 4IR, and analysis of data from online job portals from each country to assess trends in skills demand. The study used a modeling exercise to estimate job displacement and gains in the selected industries in each of the countries. A review of the policy landscape based on benchmarks from international trends and experiences provides the basis for the action points that countries can use to harness the potential of Industry 4.0 to increase productivity, facilitate skills development, and incentivize industry.

The findings and recommendations from the study point us to collaborate with our partners to implement decisive changes in renewing skills development strategies that acquire a full life cycle approach to skills development. This means that there are no degrees or certificates for life and constant renewals and upskilling are essential. The preponderant focus on institution-based training needs to give way to more flexible and multimodal training to include bootcamps, e-learning, and work-place based training. Training for digital skills at basic, intermediate, and higher levels needs a significant ramp up as workplaces undergo digital transformation.

As co-team leaders, we thank the consultant team led by Fraser Thompson, director, AlphaBeta, for an excellent partnership in this study. The core team in AlphaBeta include Konstantin Matthies, engagement manager; Genevieve Lim, engagement manager; and Richard McClellan, senior advisor. We thank AlphaBeta's national experts Ananto Kusuma Seta (Indonesia), Dao Quang Vinh (Viet Nam), Jose Roland A. Moya (Philippines), and Trevor Sworn (Cambodia). AlphaBeta's team developed the analytical model for the study and collaborated closely with ADB's team to bring new insights and directions and we are grateful for this professional collaboration.

Brajesh Panth, Ayako Inagaki, Robert Guild, and Rana Hasan provided valuable guidance to the study. We thank Shamit Chakravarti, Lynette Perez, Yumiko Yamakawa, and Sakiko Tanaka in ADB's Southeast Asia Human and Social Development Division and Paul Vandenberg and Elisabetta Gentile from the Economic Research and Regional Cooperation Department for providing inputs at various stages of the study and Sophea Mar, Sutarum Wiryono, Vinh Ngo from ADB resident missions in Cambodia, Indonesia, and Viet Nam, respectively, for their valuable support and country-level consultations. Iris Miranda, Sheela Rances, and Dorothy Geronimo from ADB, and Jannis Hoh, Shivin Kohli, and Anna Lim from AlphaBeta provided timely coordination of meetings and activities during the study. We thank April Gallega for coordinating the editing of the reports for publication and Mike Cortes for the cover designs.

The study would not have been possible if not for the leadership of senior government and industry representatives and senior members of the academia in the respective countries. We were heartened to note the high level of interest on the topic of 4IR. In each of the countries, there are already several important initiatives underway to enable industry and companies to move toward application of 4IR. The study was closely coordinated with senior government and industry participants, specifically on the selection of the two sectors for detailed study for each of the countries. The emerging findings of the study were shared in country level workshops. Senior officials and key counterparts consulted are listed at the end of each country report.

We look forward to discussions in taking forward the study's policy recommendations.

Shanti Jagannathan
Principal Education Specialist
Sustainable Development
and Climate Change Department

Sameer Khatiwada
Social Sector Specialist
South East Asia Department

Abbreviations

4IR	Industry 4.0 or Fourth Industrial Revolution
ADB	Asian Development Bank
AI	artificial intelligence
ASEAN	Association of Southeast Asian Nations
ICT	information and communication technology
ILO	International Labour Organization
ITM	industry transformation map
MSMEs	micro, small, and medium-sized enterprises
STEP	Systematic Tracking of Exchanges in Procurement
TVET	technical and vocational education and training

Executive Summary

Background of the Study

The future of jobs is at the heart of the development conundrum in developing countries in the Asia and Pacific region in the coming years, and preparing the workforce of the future with the right skills and capabilities is central to the technical and vocational education and training (TVET) and skills development portfolio of the Asian Development Bank (ADB). In recent years, disruptive technologies have intensified worries around extensive job losses arising from automation and potential disappearance of the comparative advantage of countries based on competitive labor costs. Hence, the readiness of developing countries to effectively transition to Industry 4.0 or the Fourth Industrial Revolution (4IR), has become an area of concern. To understand the implications of 4IR on the future of jobs and to prepare education and training institutions for labor markets, ADB undertook a study to capture the anticipated transformations of jobs, tasks, and skills and to outline policy directions to prepare the workforce for the future.

Scope of the Study

The study covers Cambodia, Indonesia, the Philippines, and Viet Nam and includes the following features:

(i)   Focus on two industries per country deemed important for growth, employment, and 4IR: tourism and garments (Cambodia); food and beverages, and automotive manufacturing (Indonesia); information technology and business process outsourcing (or IT-BPO) and electronics manufacturing (Philippines); and agro-processing and logistics (Viet Nam).

(ii)   Survey of employers in the chosen industries, a modeling exercise to estimate job displacements and gains, a survey of training institutions on their readiness for 4IR, and analysis of data from online job portals from each of the countries to assess skills demand trends.

(iii)   Assessment of the policy landscape for harnessing the potential of 4IR to increase productivity, facilitate skills development, and incentivize industry based on benchmarks derived from international trends and experiences.

(iv)   Recommendations to strengthen policy approaches to 4IR, particularly keeping in mind the investments needed for new approaches to skills and training, and the strategies and actions needed to prepare the country's workforce for 4IR.

The COVID-19 Effect

The study was undertaken and completed prior to the spread of the coronavirus disease (COVID-19), which has caused unprecedented disruptions to labor markets and to the activities of the global workforce. This study's policy recommendations and strategies to strengthen widespread digital capabilities, enhance online/distance learning, digital platforms, education technology (or edtech), and simulation-based learning have become even more relevant in the aftermath of COVID-19. The key approaches discussed in the report bear great relevance to the current context of countries experiencing nationwide closures of schools and training institutes. The expectation is also that, post-COVID-19, there will be operating procedures in the workplace that constitute a "new normal" and will require enhanced digital capabilities. Hence, the findings of this study and the follow-on policy directions are very timely and crucial for facilitating a sustainable COVID-19 recovery strategy.

The two sectors chosen for the study in Viet Nam, agro-processing and logistics, have been adversely affected by the pandemic. In agro-processing, because of the pervasive impact on supply chains and value chains, the industry will need to rethink potential lasting shifts in consumer behavior in dealing with the COVID-19 response. Food retailers are likely to scale up e-commerce. The logistics part of the sector is likely to become more tech-oriented, calling for new skills and talent. More broadly, the logistics sector is expected to experience a significant upswing after COVID-19, arising from the growth of e-commerce and the changing nature of retail business due to the pandemic. Recovery from COVID-19 will entail embracing digital supply chains and launching digital sales and marketing initiatives. Hence, the upskilling and reskilling on 4IR-related occupations is even more urgent for the revival of the economy and economic stimulus needed post-COVID-19.

The study obviously does not address the implications of COVID-19 in Viet Nam; however, the policy directions and future investments for higher order skills, particularly in the digital domain, are eminently suitable for the country to reimagine new beginnings for the two sectors.

Key Findings

As the study covered four countries in Southeast Asia, a report has been prepared for each—Cambodia, Indonesia, the Philippines, and Viet Nam. A synthesis report compiling key findings and a comparative picture across these countries is also available. This report covers the key findings of the study for Viet Nam. The logistics and agro-processing industries were selected for an analysis of the implications of 4IR for jobs, tasks, and skills in Viet Nam. These industries hold importance for national employment, growth, international competitiveness, and relevance for 4IR technologies. The logistics (proxied by data provided for the industry classification "Transportation and Storage") industry accounted for 3.3% of total employment and 2.9% of gross domestic product in 2017, and 1.8% of total exports in 2016; the agro-processing industry accounted for 5.8% of total employment in 2016, and 15% of gross domestic product in 2018, and food products accounted for 2.7% of total exports while textiles accounted for 16.3%.

The study finds that 4IR will have a transformational effect on jobs and skills in both industries, with great potential for jobs and productivity that can be reaped through adequate investments in skills and training. Key findings from the study include:

   (i)   **4IR will bring both job displacement and job gains.**
         (a) Application of 4IR technologies will lead to a loss of jobs arising from automation;
             however, it could also lead to new labor demand through productivity increases, and the

study estimates a positive net effect on jobs in both industries. While 26% of the current workforce in logistics and 33% of those in agro-processing could potentially be displaced by 4IR technologies, there will also be additional demand. It is estimated that there will be additional labor demand in the logistics (by 38%) and agro-processing (by 68%) industries leading to positive job gains.

(b) Significant productivity improvements are expected in both industries with the application of 4IR technologies. The study reports that 41% of employers in logistics and 31% of those in agro-processing, expect productivity improvements of over 25% from the application of 4IR technologies by 2030. However, it is also acknowledged that the cost of adopting 4IR technology is high.

(c) The study warns that there are no guarantees that displaced workers can seamlessly move into new jobs that will emerge from productivity increases, without adequate and timely investments in skills development.

(ii) **Jobs will shift from routine, physical tasks to higher order tasks with 4IR.**

(a) The research indicates an increase in the time spent on nonroutine tasks, as well as analytical tasks across both industries. In both industries, there would likely be large decreases in the time that workers spend on routine physical tasks. For example, for agro-processing, by 2030, workers could be spending over 12% less time in a working week on routine physical tasks with 4IR.

(b) With diminishing manual and physical activities in a 4IR workplace, skills such as evaluation, judgment, and decision-making are expected to become far more important in both industries by 2030. Surveyed employers, as well as information from online job portals, illustrate the growing importance of such skills compared to routine physical and just technical skills.

(iii) **Skills shortages and inadequate skill levels in both industries need to be addressed.**

(a) While preparing the workforce for 4IR, it is important to address the overall skills shortages and a lack of preparation of people for the workplace. Over 60% of employers in the logistics and agro-processing industries reported that graduates hired in the past year have not been adequately prepared by their pre-hire education and/or training.

(b) Employers in both industries stress the importance of training and skills development in preparation for 4IR. On-the-job training will be crucial to deliver the required skill shift. The logistics industry will require close to 37 million additional person trainings while the agro-processing industry will need 33 million additional person-trainings (one-person training refers to training one worker, in one skill from the average level required by their occupation in their industry in 2018 to the required level in 2030) by 2030. Education and training institutions also need to augment preparation of graduates for entry level positions.

(iv) **Training institutions in Viet Nam need to prepare for the challenges of 4IR**

(a) There is strong alignment between the skills that training institutions believe will be particularly important due to 4IR and the perceptions of employers in the logistics and agro-processing industries. However, some training institutions may be struggling to keep pace with the rate of change in skills demand. For example, 47% of training institutions surveyed review and update their curricula less than annually, and less than half of institutions provide information on job market conditions to their students.

(b) Engagement with business also appears to be strong, with 43% of training institutions stating that they communicate and coordinate with employers in relevant industries several times a year and 22% stating that they engage on a monthly basis (or even more regularly).

Of all training institutions, 77% reported working with employers on curriculum input, while 73% reported that they organize internships, with over 60% organizing workplace-based training, job fairs, and train-the-teacher programs. However, the study suggests that there is a need to evaluate the quality of such partnerships.

(c) Despite the reported close engagement with industry, the study finds a significant mismatch in the perceptions on skill preparation between employers and training institutions. While 80% of training institutions believe that their graduates are well-prepared for the 4IR workforce, only 37% of employers in logistics and 39% agro-processing.

(d) Of the surveyed training institutions, 56% reported that they already have dedicated programs related to 4IR skills; 71% reported plans to develop or expand programs for 4IR by 2025. While this is an encouraging trend, it is critical to assess the quality and relevance of such training and their alignment with employer needs. A structured needs assessment for training for 4IR is needed, as almost 80% of training institutions surveyed stated that additional financial and technical support is needed.

(v) **Courses and training delivery have begun to change but further transformation is needed.**

(a) The study finds promising self-reported trends in training institutions of adopting technology for teaching and learning, particularly digital training. Over half reported using interactive videos. However, the deployment of advanced technologies is still limited— only 4% of training institutions have adopted virtual learning platforms. The quality and standards used in these new tools are also yet to be ascertained.

(b) Training institutions have a strong focus on instructor and teacher assessment. However, exposure of teachers and trainers to the workplace appears limited. Of the surveyed training institutions, 80% have annual or semi-annual performance reviews for teachers, but only 52% provide teachers with on-the-job time devoted to gaining practical knowledge and new teaching techniques.

(vi) **Viet Nam's 4IR policies and strategies are in the right direction and need active implementation.**

(a) Viet Nam's 4IR strategy is a work in progress. The Central Institute for Economic Management is finalizing a comprehensive national strategy; a first draft has been completed, but it has not been made publicly available, so as of writing there is no formal direction or policy on 4IR. Where there are directives, decisions, and policies relevant to future skills and/or 4IR, they tend to offer only high-level guidance without much specificity (e.g., urging leaders at all levels to improve awareness of job opportunities coming from vocational education).

(b) There are also gaps in key policy areas related to 4IR, including the lack of awareness of in-demand jobs and skills and the lack of strong incentives for firms to invest in relevant training.

(c) Greater efforts are needed to promote inclusiveness linked to 4IR. There are large gaps in training of employees in urban areas (30.9%) versus rural areas (9.0%). Given the currently limited social protection even for regular workers, there is still some way to go to protect on-demand, or flexible workers in the new economy.

Key Recommendations and Way Forward

To address current gaps in policy actions and enhance the effectiveness of implementation mechanisms, seven recommendations have been identified for Viet Nam to strengthen its preparedness toward 4IR. A multi-stakeholder approach to the actions in each of these recommendations will be critical to their effectiveness. For each, a potential lead from either the government or private sector has been identified, alongside a list of stakeholders suggested to be engaged when developing and implementing the recommended actions. These recommended actions include:

(i) **Develop 4IR transformation roadmaps for key sectors.** As the 4IR strategy is launched by Viet Nam, a practical starting point for its implementation could be to develop Singapore-style Industry Transformation Maps, which provide information on technology impacts, career pathways, and the skills required for different occupations and reskilling options for different industries. Industry-specific roadmaps for the logistics and agro-processing industries could be a useful starting point. This would include the creation of skills councils, i.e., employer-led organizations that would support the development of occupational standards and qualifications frameworks in different industries.

(ii) **Develop a series of industry-led TVET programs targeting skills for 4IR.** Building on ongoing efforts to improve linkages between TVET and industry, Viet Nam could develop programs specifically for 4IR, including new courses, credentials, and quality assurance mechanisms. The initial focus could be on the logistics and agro-processing industries. The McKinsey-founded independent nonprofit Generation is a good example of an industry-led program. Over 30,000 people from 13 countries have graduated from its programs. Of this number, 81% were employed within 3 months after graduation and received salaries two to six times higher than their previous earnings.

(iii) **Upgrade training delivery through 4IR technology in classrooms and training facilities.** Technology adoption in the classroom in Viet Nam for the world of 4IR appears limited. Greater deployment of new technologies such as virtual reality, augmented reality, and simulation would strengthen workforce readiness. Given the substantial need for on-the-job training, it is recommended to explore potential digital platforms to deliver skills development at scale. These new approaches need to permeate high schools, TVET institutions, polytechnics, and higher education institutions. Preparation of a systematic suite of 4IR methodologies for use in training delivery would be valuable.

(iv) **Develop flexible and modular skill certification programs.** It is recommended that Viet Nam develop flexible certification programs that recognize skills attainment outside traditional education channels. A good example of a skill-based accreditation system is the Malaysian Skills Certification Program, under which skill certificates are granted to workers who do not have any formal educational qualifications but who have obtained relevant knowledge, experience, and skills in the workplace to enhance their career prospects.

(v) **Build programs to raise awareness of reskilling benefits, critical skills, and training opportunities.** Besides the benefits of reskilling, it is also important that workers and employers are informed about the requisite skills and how to leverage them. This could include developing real-time online information and mobile applications on in-demand skills (similar to New Zealand's "Occupation Outlook") and developing an outreach program to inform workers and employers of available skills training and support. For example, the Government of Singapore has established a dedicated unit to reach out to firms and educate them about worker reskilling needs and opportunities under the government's skills training courses.

(vi) **Implement an incentive scheme for firms to train employees for 4IR.** There are minimal private sector incentives to invest in skills development in Viet Nam due to market failures relating to information asymmetries. A starting point to address these incentives could be to survey employers regarding more investment in training, and to test a range of incentives, including tax relief in exchange for employees going through training programs (whether through TVET, third-party training institutes, or in-house) or offering delivery of TVET programs on-site for large employers. The cost-benefit of each scheme would then need to be rigorously assessed before being piloted.

(vii) **Formulate new approaches and measures to strengthen inclusion and social protection in the context of 4IR.** It is critical to ensure that the country's journey toward 4IR includes providing opportunities to the underprivileged. Support for three types of workers is needed: entry level workers, workers at risk of job displacement, and workers needing upskilling. Modern delivery mechanisms, including digital platforms with industry-recognized credentials can reach the underprivileged in remote locations. Viet Nam could analyze variations in access to critical skills by age, gender, geography, and economic background. This could then inform the targeted training programs, which could be developed in conjunction with the private sector. For example, Microsoft has established several targeted programs that address the relative disadvantages faced by at-risk youth, women, long-term unemployed individuals, and people with disabilities.

While these recommendations apply to both the logistics and agro-processing industries, there are a set of priorities unique to each industry that should be considered when implementing the respective actions. These include:

(i) **Logistics.** Leverage the growth of the local e-commerce industry to build 4IR readiness, improve the capacity of employers to deliver on-the-job training, and develop a standardized set of 4IR skills requirements and training curricula.

(ii) **Agro-processing.** Address the disproportionate impact of technological disruption on females; enhance employers' knowledge of 4IR technologies; and support 4IR knowledge transfer from large companies to micro, small, and medium-sized enterprises.

CHAPTER 1

The Industry 4.0 Skills Challenge

This chapter investigates the supply and demand of skills driven by Industry 4.0 (4IR) technology adoption for both the logistics and agro-processing industries in Viet Nam. The analysis utilized a range of data, including employer surveys and interviews, online job board data, and national labor market statistics.

In both industries, the impact of 4IR will be transformative for jobs and skills. The analysis shows that despite widespread concerns of significant automation and loss of jobs associated with 4IR, the net impact on jobs for both industries to 2030 is likely to be positive, with more jobs being created than displaced. However, there are no guarantees that displaced workers can seamlessly move into these new jobs, as they will likely lack the relevant skills. While the overall patterns of impact in the two industries are similar, there are some important differences. The displacement of jobs in the agro-processing industry is far larger than the logistics sector and could particularly impact women. Of the total jobs that could be displaced in agro-processing by 2030, 64% are currently held by women.

In terms of skills, judgment and decision-making will become more important by 2030 in both industries, but the agro-processing industry will also require significant increases in technical skills. There is also a greater need for advanced level skills in agro-processing versus logistics.

By 2030, the logistics industry will require over 37 million additional person trainings and the agro-processing industry will need 33 million.[1] In the logistics industry, 65% of this skill gap will have to be addressed on the job, meaning the technical and vocational education and training (TVET) sector will have to increasingly play a role in these forms of trainings. In the agro-processing industry, longer formal trainings will also be of crucial importance, allowing for a more traditional TVET approach.

Industry 4.0 and the Relevance for Viet Nam

4IR is a widely used but often misunderstood term that refers to a range of new technologies impacting the workplace. The term was first conceptualized to describe data exchange technologies used in manufacturing. However, the term has now been given a broader meaning (and sometimes referred to as the Fourth Industrial Revolution), where it refers to technologies applied across all sectors that combine the physical, digital, and biological worlds.[2] These technologies include cyber-physical systems, the Internet of Things (IoT), Artificial Intelligence (AI), cloud computing, and cognitive computing.

---

[1]   One-person training refers to training one worker, in one skill from the average level required by their occupation in their industry in 2018 to the required level in 2030.

[2]   K. Schwab. 2017. *The Fourth Industrial Revolution*. New York: Currency. https://books.google.com.sg/books?hl=en&lr=&id=ST_FDAA AQBAJ&oi=fnd&pg=PR7&dq=klaus+schwab+fourth+industrial+revolution&ots=DTnvbTqvTQ&sig=aOLqcUCFsLKbNpjWa5kr2Sjz hu4#v=onepage&q=klaus%20schwab%20fourth%20industrial%20revolution&f=false.

4IR is a very different concept from previous industrial revolutions, both in terms of scope and technologies (Figure 1). The First Industrial Revolution in the 18th century was marked by a transition from hand production methods to machines through the use of steam power and water power. The Second Industrial Revolution occurred in the 19th century and involved the use of extensive railroad networks and the telegraph to allow faster transfer of people and ideas, combined with factory electrification and the creation of mass production assembly line approaches. The Third Industrial Revolution occurred in the late 20th century and is often referred to as the digital revolution, involving the use of computers and the Internet, robots and automation, and electronics. 4IR builds on these past industrial revolutions, but includes a far broader array of technologies with applicability across all industries. In this regard, it is fundamentally different from the past industrial revolutions in its potential implications for economies and the workforce.

Figure 1: What is Industry 4.0?

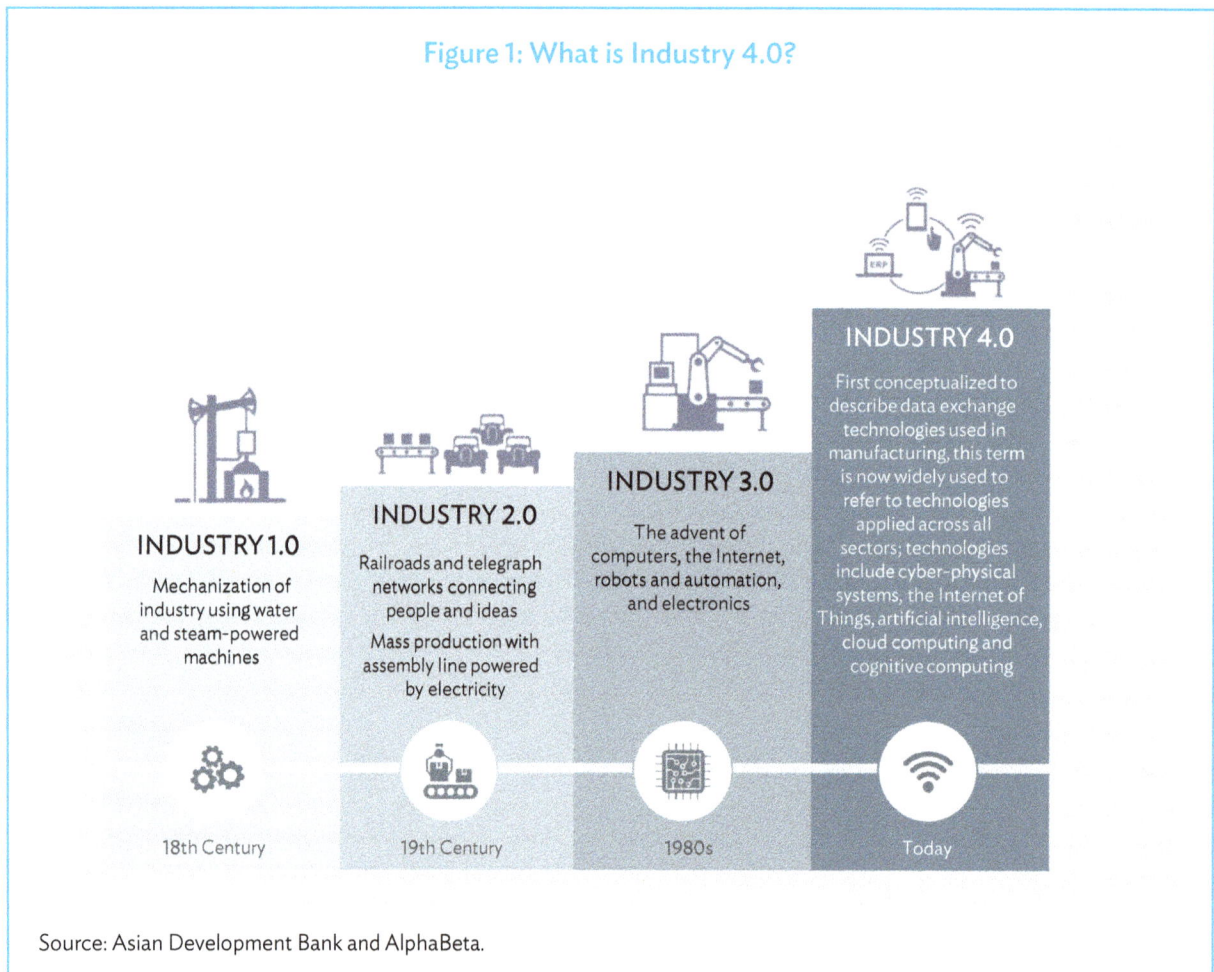

INDUSTRY 1.0

Mechanization of industry using water and steam-powered machines

18th Century

INDUSTRY 2.0

Railroads and telegraph networks connecting people and ideas

Mass production with assembly line powered by electricity

19th Century

INDUSTRY 3.0

The advent of computers, the Internet, robots and automation, and electronics

1980s

INDUSTRY 4.0

First conceptualized to describe data exchange technologies used in manufacturing, this term is now widely used to refer to technologies applied across all sectors; technologies include cyber-physical systems, the Internet of Things, artificial intelligence, cloud computing and cognitive computing

Today

Source: Asian Development Bank and AlphaBeta.

What could 4IR mean for Viet Nam? According to the Central Institute for Economic Management (CIEM), 4IR technology could increase Viet Nam's gross domestic product by between $28.5 billion and $62 billion by 2030, equivalent to a rise of 7%–16%, compared to 2018, as a result of increased productivity and employment opportunities. One key driver of this large upside opportunity is limited digital adoption to date. In 2018, the World Bank scored Viet Nam at 0.46 out of 1.00 on its Digital Adoption Index, behind fellow Association of Southeast Asian Nations (ASEAN) member states Singapore, Malaysia, and Thailand; however, for business digital adoption, Viet Nam scored second to last out of the seven ASEAN member states assessed.[3] Recent research by the United Nations Development Programme (UNDP) confirms that 85% of industrial enterprises in Viet Nam remain outsiders to 4IR.[4] By contrast, Viet Nam appears to be well prepared for 4IR from an employee skill level. According to a 4IR readiness assessment conducted by the Ministry of Industry and Trade and UNDP, the "employee skills" score was significantly above other measures of readiness.

With the large potential of 4IR, it is only understandable that there are concerns about the impact on employment from such new technologies. Most concerns revolve around fears that 4IR could lead to mass unemployment as (i) workers are replaced by machines; or (ii) workers do not have the right skills to effectively work alongside 4IR technologies or transition into new emerging jobs. These fears are exacerbated by how, according to recent research, only 2%–4% of enterprises have sufficiently equipped employees with knowledge and skills to cope with 4IR (footnote 4).

Understanding how the skills landscape is likely to change under 4IR is becoming harder in the face of the rapid pace at which technology is developing and being adopted. This means traditional approaches of assessing skill gaps, often relying on time-intensive processes to collect data that quickly become outdated, may no longer be suitable. This study explores a new innovative approach to understanding the labor market implications of 4IR that tries to address gaps in previous studies. Some key design aspects of the methodology include:

(i) **Use of local data.** This study utilizes a variety of local data sources, including the Viet Nam national labor force survey, the World Bank's Skills Measurement Program (STEP) survey for Viet Nam, as well as surveys of Vietnamese businesses in the logistics and agro-processing industries.

(ii) **Use of current market information.** Given the rapid change in the labor market, existing labor market surveys can become quickly obsolete. To address this concern, this report utilizes information on skill profiles for current occupations advertised in online job portals in Viet Nam.

(iii) **Focus on supply, not just demand.** Much of the past research has examined only changes in occupations and skills related to 4IR. This study aims to go further by examining the supply landscape, including understanding the volume and types of training required and conducting a survey of current training institutes in Viet Nam to understand the degree to which they are currently addressing the shifts in demand for skills being seen in this analysis.

3   O. Dione. 2018. 4IR – Harnessing Disruption for Viet Nam's Development. *World Bank: Speeches & Transcripts.* https://www.worldbank.org/en/news/speech/2018/07/13/industry-4-harnessing-disruption-for-Viet Nams-development.

4   Ministry of Industry and Trade, UNDP. 2019. *4IR Readiness of Industry Enterprises in Viet Nam.* https://www.vn.undp.org/content/Viet Nam/en/home/library/I40.html.

Industry Selection

Two industries were chosen to conduct this analysis of 4IR implications for the demand and supply of skills. A two-step methodology was used to select the industries:

  (i)   **Shortlisting industries prioritized by the Government of Viet Nam for future growth or for 4IR application.** This included reviewing the Five-Year Socio-Economic Development Plan 2016–2020 and the Industrial Development Strategy through 2025, vision to 2035.
  (ii) **Scoring and ranking shortlisted industries according to a set of criteria:**
        (a) How significant is the industry's contribution to the country's employment?
        (b) Does it exhibit strong recent employment growth?
        (c) Are its exports internationally competitive?
        (d) Is 4IR of relevance to the industry?
        (e) Are relevant data available for the industry analysis?

The industries were then tested with various stakeholders during a country consultation in July 2019. Based on this process, the logistics and agro-processing industry were selected for the analysis.

  (i)   **Logistics.** The logistics industry is a significant contributor to employment in Viet Nam. According to the International Labour Organization and Viet Nam's Statistical Yearbook 2017, the transportation and storage industry contributed 3.3% to total employment in 2017 and employment grew by 4.56% annually from 2015–2017.[5] However, logistics costs in Viet Nam remain higher than the ASEAN average, which in turn can impact Viet Nam's international competitiveness.[6] Recent data suggest some signs of improvement. For example, in the World Bank's Logistics Performance Index, Viet Nam ranked 39th out of 160 countries in 2018, a 25-rank improvement since 2016.[7] 4IR technologies could significantly improve the performance of the logistics industry. 4IR components—like product classification, labelling and arrangement, or automatic monitoring of inventory—will be crucial as the supply chains mature in Viet Nam. This industry is also strategically important to fuel further growth in other industries as it is heavily integrated into Viet Nam's rapidly growing sectors, including e-commerce.
  (ii) **Agro-processing.** The agro-processing industry encompasses early stages of the production value chain for the manufacture of food products, beverages, tobacco products, textiles, leather and related products, wood and products of wood and cork, as well as paper and paper products. Data from the General Statistics Office indicate that the agro-processing industry represented 5.8% of Viet Nam's total employment in 2016. The actual activities for these manufacturing subsectors that could be described as agro-processing may be closer to 4.5% of all jobs in the economy of Viet Nam (equivalent to about 31% of industrial jobs).[8] The industry is also showing strong growth (employment has grown annually by 5.3% from

5   International Labour Organization. 2020. https://www.ilo.org/global/lang--en/index.htm; Viet Nam. General Statistics Office. 2017. Statistical Yearbook of Viet Nam. https://web.archive.org/web/20190313120427/http://www.gso.gov.vn/default_en.aspx?tabid=515&idmid=5&ItemID=18941.

6   V. L. Dang and G. T. Yeo. 2018. Weighing the Key Factors to Improve Viet Nam's Logistics System. *The Asian Journal of Shipping and Logistics*, https://www.sciencedirect.com/science/article/pii/S2092521218300774; World Bank. 2014. *Efficient Logistics – A Key to Viet Nam's Competitiveness*, http://documents.worldbank.org/curated/en/646871468132885170/pdf/Efficient-logistics-a-key-to-Viet Nams-competitiveness.pdf.

7   World Bank. 2018. LPI Index. https://lpi.worldbank.org/international/global/2018.

8   World Bank. 2018. *Viet Nam's Future Jobs: Leveraging Mega-Trends for Greater Prosperity*. https://www.worldbank.org/en/country/Viet Nam/publication/Viet Nam-future-jobs-leveraging-mega-trends-for-greater-prosperity.

2014–2016 on average). According to Viet Nam's Industrial Development Strategy, in the period to 2025, raising the proportion of processing of key agricultural products in accordance with the restructuring of the agricultural sector will be prioritized. Viet Nam is looking to apply international standards for processing agricultural products, thus building trademarks and improving competitiveness. Agro-processing is currently underdeveloped in Viet Nam and 4IR technologies could create an opportunity for it to move up the value chain from simply focusing on raw produce and primary agriculture. Dairy processing is already emerging as a strong, end-to-end value chain in Viet Nam, and others are likely to follow. The close link to agriculture also means that agro-processing could combat the decline in employment seen in agriculture.[9]

Logistics Industry

The logistics industry stands to be a major beneficiary of 4IR, with productivity benefits driven by a range of different technologies. However, 4IR technology adoption is likely going to lead to significant job displacement in the short run, with 26% of all jobs affected. The challenge will be to redirect these workers into new occupations, as well as provide them with the right skills to continue in their occupations in an 4IR-dominated landscape. To achieve this, a significant amount of additional training between 2018 and 2030 will be required. Over 60% of this training will need to be provided on-the-job.

Relevance of 4IR

4IR technology in the logistics sector is being driven by several macroeconomic trends. These include:

(i) **Global supply chains.** Increasingly globalized supply chains require more complex management to understand how to manage stock levels and keep track of goods in transit.

(ii) **Changing consumer trends.** Consumers are increasingly demanding more customization of products and faster turnaround times, which in turn places pressures on logistics systems.

(iii) **Greater focus on reliability of production and transport systems.** As facilities increasingly move toward 24-hour production, equipment reliability becomes even more critical. 4IR-enabled warehouses have robust monitoring systems to identify potential maintenance issues before they cause downtime.[10]

(iv) **Challenges in workforce availability.** One of the biggest challenges facing the logistics industry today is labor availability. The e-commerce revolution is rapidly increasing demand for logistics; however, the available workforce is not able to keep pace.[11]

---

[9]   World Bank. 2018. *Viet Nam's Future Jobs: Leveraging Mega-Trends for Greater Prosperity.* https://www.worldbank.org/en/country/Viet Nam/publication/Viet Nam-future-jobs-leveraging-mega-trends-for-greater-prosperity.

[10] K. Masters. 2017. *The Impact of Industry 4.0 on the Automotive Industry.* https://blog.flexis.com/the-impact-of-industry-4.0-on-the-automotive-industry.

[11] DHL. 2016. *Robotics in Logistics.* https://www.dhl.com/content/dam/downloads/g0/about_us/logistics_insights/dhl_trendreport_robotics.pdf.

There are various specific 4IR technologies for the logistics sector, ranging from digital technologies enabling smart factories through to IoT technology to provide real-time information on products. Some key technologies include:

(i)   **Internet of Things.** IoT refers to networks of sensors and actuators embedded in machines and other physical objects that connect with one another and the Internet. It has a wide range of applications, including data collection, monitoring, decision-making, and process optimization.[12] DHL predicts that IoT technology will represent nearly a $2 billion opportunity for the logistics industry, including smart warehousing, real-time transport, and predictive delivery.[13] For example, radio frequency identification (RFID) tags on containers can track products as they move from the factory to stores, allowing companies to avoid stock-outs and losses. Singapore's YCH Group reduced stock turnaround time by 20% in a 220,000 square foot warehouse of close to 3,000 stock-keeping units by using RFID systems for more accurate pallet sorting.[14]

(ii) **Blockchain technology.** Blockchain technology refers to a list of public records, also known as a public ledger, where transactions between parties are listed or stored. Each record, known as a "block" within blockchain terminology, is secured using cryptography. Blockchain can make accessing and storing important information easier and more reliable (e.g., payment information, status of deliveries), because responsibility for storing it is shared across the whole network.[15]

(iii) **Artificial intelligence and big data.** Big data refers to the ability to analyze extremely large volumes of data, extract insights, and act on them closer to real time. This has a range of benefits in the logistics sector, including being able to use predictive analytics to finetune production volumes and processes and better supply chain management. For example, order picking is one of the most important process steps in logistics. User studies performed in storage environments have shown Augmented Reality can improve processes on a big scale.[16]

(iv) **Industry robotics.** Industrial robots can significantly improve productivity in the logistics sector and there has been increased investment in robots in this sector in response to drivers such as wage costs, 24x7 production requirements, and high levels of staff turnover. Robots are increasingly being used for functions ranging from forklift operations to mobile security and even using "swarm robotics" (i.e., multi-robot systems that consist of large numbers of mostly simple mobile robots) in parcel delivery (footnote 11).

(v)   **Additive manufacturing.** This describes the technologies that build 3D objects by adding layer-upon-layer of material. Additive manufacturing is potentially a threat to the logistics sector if it results in a significant shortening of the supply chain by bringing production closer to demand centers.

---

[12]   J. Woetzl et al. 2014. Southeast Asia at the Crossroads: Three Paths to Prosperity. McKinsey Global Institute. November. https://www.mckinsey.com/~/media/McKinsey/Featured%20Insights/Asia%20Pacific/Three%20paths%20to%20sustained%20economic%20growth%20in%20Southeast%20Asia/MGI%20SE%20Asia_Executive_summary_November%202014.ashx.

[13]   Robotics Business Review. 2019. Reports Indicate Strong Growth Ahead for Logistics. https://www.roboticsbusinessreview.com/supply-chain/reports-indicate-strong-growth-ahead-for-logistics/.

[14]   Honeywell Case Studies. 2010. YCH Group Selects Intermec Fixed Vehicle Computer to Improve Supply Chain Management. https://www.varinsights.com/doc/ych-group-selects-intermec-fixed-vehicle-0003.

[15]   Revfine. 2018. How Blockchain Technology Is Transforming the Travel Industry. https://www.revfine.com/blockchain-technology-travel-industry/.

[16]   R. Reif and W. Günthner. 2009. Pick-by-vision: Augmented Reality Supported Order Picking. *The Visual Computer*. https://www.researchgate.net/publication/220068297_Pick-by-vision_augmented_reality_supported_order_picking.

Adoption of 4IR technologies across the logistics industry in Viet Nam has been limited. According to World Bank research, modern supply chain technology applications have not been broadly adopted in Viet Nam.[17] However, both this and the current study show that several companies are planning to introduce many of these technologies. For example, 63% of logistics firms surveyed in Viet Nam stated that they plan to introduce technologies related to 4IR over the next 5 years (Figure 2).[18]

The impacts of 4IR technology adoption can potentially be significant. For example, international research has shown that an increase of 10% in the capital stock of AI-enabling technologies (software, databases, computer hardware, and machinery) per worker could increase labor productivity in the transport and logistics industry by 2.2%–11.4% across countries.[19] It should be noted that this research was limited to generally more developed economies, with the People's Republic of China being the closest to Viet Nam (in terms of gross domestic product per capita), where the effect of AI appears largest. This suggests that productivity impacts from 4IR could be larger for emerging economies such as Viet Nam, which aligns with the survey data, where more than 50% of employers in the logistics industry anticipated productivity improvements of 10%–50% from adopting 4IR over the next 5 years (Figure 3).

Figure 2: Sentiments Toward 4IR in the Logistics Industry in Viet Nam

Logistics: 4IR readiness

Companies in the logistics industry claim to have a good understanding of 4IR technologies and more than 60% have adoption plans

Respondents (%)

Legend: Don't know | Disagree | Agree | Strongly disagree | Neither agree nor disagree | Strongly agree

Statement	Don't know	Strongly disagree	Disagree	Neither agree nor disagree	Agree	Strongly agree
I have a good understanding of 4IR technologies and their relevance for my company	15	2	8	17	25	10
My company already adopts 4IR technologies in our operations		1	18	21	42	4
My company plans to adopt 4IR technologies in our operations by 2025	10	1	6	20	48	15
The cost of 4IR technologies is a significant barrier to adoption for our company	10	1%	8	20	48	13

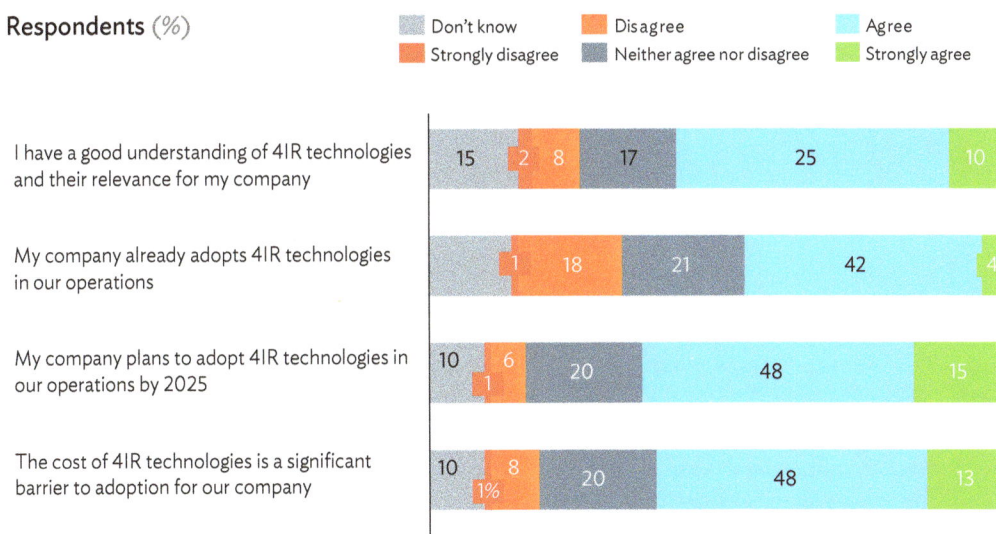

4IR = Industry 4.0 or Fourth Industrial Revolution.

Source: Employer survey on impact of 4IR on the logistics industry in Viet Nam, n=84.

---

[17]   World Bank. 2019. *Viet Nam: Assessment of Logistics Skills, Training, and Competencies of Male and Female Employees.*
[18]   Based on 84 completed responses.
[19]   PWC. 2018. *The Macroeconomic Impact of Artificial Intelligence.* https://www.pwc.co.uk/economic-services/assets/macroeconomic-impact-of-ai-technical-report-feb-18.pdf.

Figure 3: Expected Productivity Improvement Due to 4IR Technologies

Logistics: Productivity

More than 50% of employers in the logistics industry in Viet Nam expect
a 10%–50%productivity increase from 4IR technologies over the next 5 years

Respondents (%)

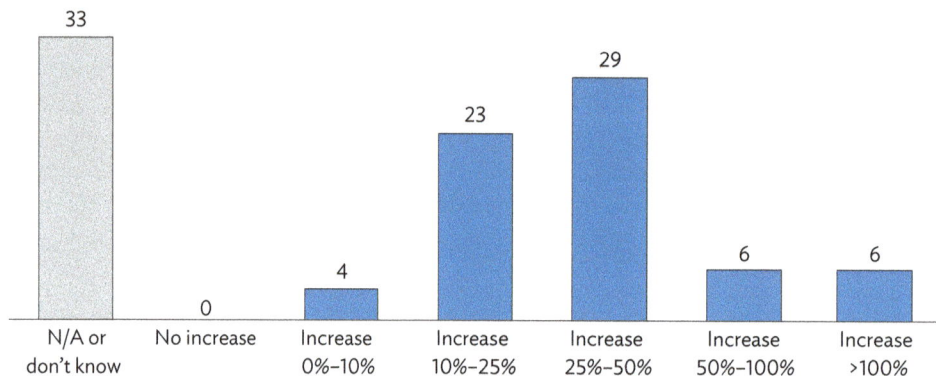

4IR = Industry 4.0 or Fourth Industrial Revolution.

Source: Employer survey on impact of 4IR on the logistics industry in Viet Nam, n=84.

Skills Demand Analysis

Employment Implications

The analysis examines two factors influencing employment in the logistics sector related to 4IR:

(i) **Displacement effect.** This refers to the number of jobs lost due to the automation of tasks through the application 4IR technology. Job displacement occurs only if tasks automated by technology make up such a significant proportion of time spent at work, or if such tasks are so essential that a worker is no longer needed. The analysis estimates this displacement at 17% of today's employment, equivalent to over 540,000 workers.

(ii) **Income effect.** The income effect refers to the additional demand for labor driven by the improvement to productivity from 4IR technologies. As 4IR makes the existing workforce more productive, the cost of production and by extension, the price of products, can fall. This increases demand and hence, labor.

Contrary to some perceptions that 4IR will lead to mass unemployment, the research provides an overall optimistic assessment (Figure 4). Net employment from 4IR may actually rise in the logistics sector as displacement effects from 4IR are offset by employment linked to productivity gains (i.e., the income effect).

However, even though the overall impact on employment appears to be positive, this does not mean that 4IR could not lead to substantial numbers of workers losing their jobs. There are four critical challenges to realizing the theoretical positive income effect:

Figure 4: Impact of 4IR on Number of Jobs in Viet Nam's Logistics Industry, 2018–2030 (%)

Logistics: Jobs

The overall impact of 4IR on jobs is likely to be limited as negative displacement effects are potentially offset by large positive income effects

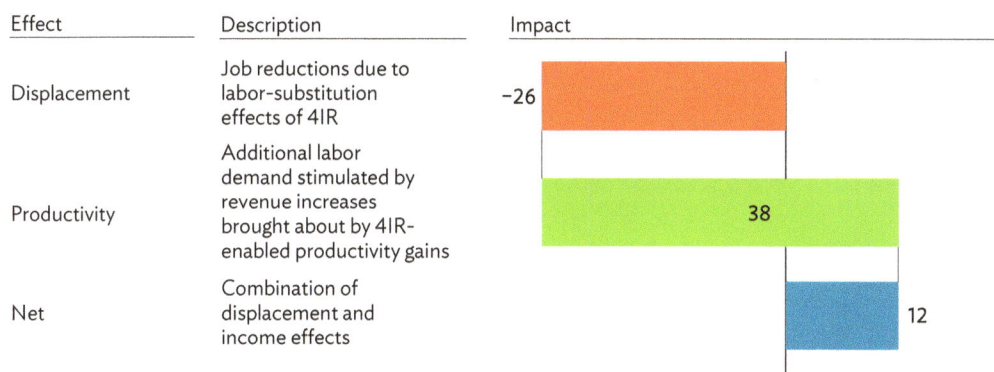

Effect	Description	Impact
Displacement	Job reductions due to labor-substitution effects of 4IR	−26
Productivity	Additional labor demand stimulated by revenue increases brought about by 4IR-enabled productivity gains	38
Net	Combination of displacement and income effects	12

4IR = Industry 4.0 or Fourth Industrial Revolution, GDP = gross domestic product, GSO = General Statistics Office (Viet Nam), ILO = International Labour Organization, IMF = International Monetary Fund, LFS = Labour Force Surveys (Viet Nam), STEP = Systematic Tracking of Exchanges in Procurement.

Note: Change in jobs based on accelerated adoption scenario of 4IR technologies.

Sources: Industry employment – GSO, LFS 2017 and ILO; GDP/Output – GSO and IMF Article IV; STEP survey data; Employer survey on impact of 4IR on the logistics industry in Viet Nam, n= 57+; Job portal data: jobs in the logistics industry scraped from the job portal VietnamWorks over the period from July to August 2019.

(i)   There is no guarantee that the 26% of workers displaced will be able to seamlessly move into the 38% of jobs created. The transition may not occur if workers cannot be re-skilled accordingly.

(ii)   Furthermore, the new jobs may not materialize if there is a lack of suitable skills in the local workforce to support them. In short, Viet Nam's approach to skill development will be critical in realizing a positive labor-market outcome related to 4IR.

(iii)   There could be potential time lags to the implementation of 4IR, the job displacement, and the manifestation of productivity benefits. Hence, the productivity gains generating additional income that make new employment possible may take up to several years to materialize, reducing the positive impact by 2030.

(iv)   Some of the productivity benefits may be absorbed by companies as higher profits if industries are not competitive, or distributed to remaining workers in the form of higher wages if the supply of labor is inelastic, meaning rather than additional employment, productivity benefits could generate higher returns for existing actors in the market.

To understand what drives these results, it is important to first understand that technology does not automate jobs, but rather individual or combinations of tasks. For example, in the case of logistics, a driverless car does not replace the driver, but the task of driving and navigating on the road. The car by itself cannot replicate other tasks performed by the driver such as understanding why the car is moving from the origin to the destination, the loading and unloading of cargo, interaction with the customers sending, and receiving the cargo, etc. Box 1 describes the approach used to understand the potential employment impacts from 4IR.

Box 1: Estimating Employment Changes

This report employs an experimental approach to understanding the impact of Industry 4.0 (4IR) on employment. The core data sources used in this approach are the World Bank's Skills Measurement Program (STEP) survey for the Philippines, labor force survey data, online job portal data and surveys of employers in the prioritized industries in Viet Nam.

The trajectory of the industry is computed by looking at historic growth as a business-as-usual scenario and then modelling the impact of 4IR as a productivity shock that generates additional productivity growth. The assumption used for the estimates presented here is that adoption rates of 4IR increase to 50% until 2025 and from 2025 onward, 4IR technology adoption grows to 100% by 2030. This approach is not meant to forecast the actual, or even a necessarily realistic, level of 4IR technology adoption by 2030. Rather, it should be considered a thought experiment to understand the largest possible impact 4IR can have on employment and skills gaps. Productivity shocks and adoption levels were obtained from the employer survey and cross-referenced with the broader literature, where available.

Estimating the changes in employment across different occupations relies on a detailed analysis of "task profiles" (Box 2). The analysis identifies the changes in the time spent on particular tasks between today and a future in which 4IR has been adopted. Combining this with the breakdown of employment by occupation for the industry as well as the productivity growth estimates above, the result shows how different occupations may become more frequent in the industry. This part of the analysis mostly utilizes data from the STEP survey and Viet Nam's labor force survey.

Source: World Bank. 2019. The STEP Skills Measurement Program. https://microdata.worldbank.org/index.php/catalog/step.

Job Task Implications

The research examines five types of tasks linked to jobs in the logistics sector in Viet Nam and how they could be impacted by 4IR:

(i)   **Routine physical.** These tasks involve repetitive and predictable physical work, for example a factory worker assembling parts on a manufacturing line.

(ii) **Routine interpersonal.** These tasks involve predictable interactions with other people, for example a call center worker reading a sales script.

(iii) **Nonroutine physical.** These tasks involve physical work that is not repetitive or predictable, for example a mechanic diagnosing and repairing problems with a car engine.

(iv) **Nonroutine interpersonal.** These tasks involve complex or creative interactions with other people, for example, supervising others or making speeches or presentations.

(v)   **Analytical.** These are tasks that vary significantly and there is a strong thinking and/or analytical component. They predominantly involve computers or other technological equipment.

The research indicates an increase in the time spent on nonroutine tasks as well as analytical tasks. In fact, under an "accelerated 4IR technology adoption" scenario, workers in the sector could spend an additional 13.4% of their work week on such tasks and 13.4% less on routine physical and interpersonal tasks (Figure 5). The largest increase in time spent can be observed for nonroutine interpersonal tasks.

Figure 5: Shifts in Time Spent by Workers on Different Types of Tasks at Work in Viet Nam's Logistics Sector, 2018–2030

Logistics: Tasks

4IR in the logistics industry could lead to a shift of time spent from routine to nonroutine tasks, in particular toward nonroutine interpersonal tasks

Average share of weekly working hours spent on this task (%)

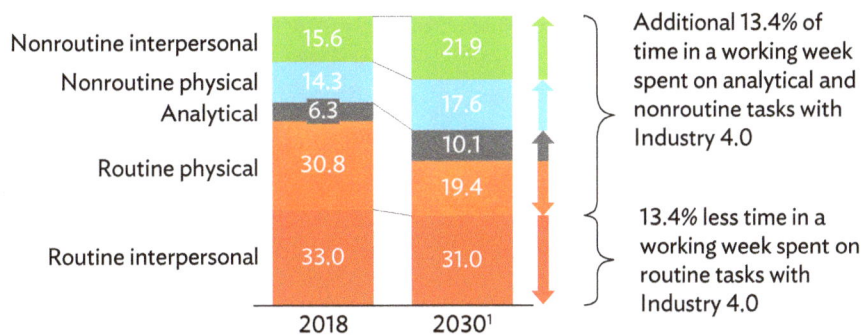

Task	2018	2030[1]
Nonroutine interpersonal	15.6	21.9
Nonroutine physical	14.3	17.6
Analytical	6.3	10.1
Routine physical	30.8	19.4
Routine interpersonal	33.0	31.0

Additional 13.4% of time in a working week spent on analytical and nonroutine tasks with Industry 4.0

13.4% less time in a working week spent on routine tasks with Industry 4.0

4IR = Industry 4.0 or Fourth Industrial Revolution, GDP = gross domestic product, GSO = General Statistics Office (Viet Nam), ILO = International Labour Organization, IMF = International Monetary Fund, LFS = Labour Force Surveys (Viet Nam), STEP = Systematic Tracking of Exchanges in Procurement.

Note: Figures include rounding adjustments.

[1] Based on "high adoption" scenario of 4IR, the Appendix has more details.

Source: Industry employment – GSO, LFS 2017 and ILO; GDP/Output – GSO and IMF Article IV; STEP survey data; Employer survey on impact of 4IR on the logistics industry in Viet Nam, n= 57+; Job portal data: jobs in the logistics industry scraped from the job portal VietnamWorks over the period from July to August 2019.

This is likely driven by how technology advances may free these workers from routine manual tasks, enabling them to spend more time on customer service-oriented tasks (e.g., delivery drivers interacting more with customers, or spending less time navigating traffic). Box 2 describes the approach used to understand the potential impacts on 4IR on tasks in the workplace.

Interestingly, the time spent on routine interpersonal tasks does not appear to be decreasing drastically, although over 60% of employers surveyed indicated that they expect the time spent on routine interpersonal tasks to decrease over the next 5 years (Figure 6). The reason for this is that even though the absolute amount of time spent on routine interpersonal tasks is decreasing, an estimated 5.4% over the next 5 years, 4IR driven productivity improvements are leading to an even faster drop in total industry hours for the existing workforce, approximately 9.2% over the same time. This means the proportion of routine interpersonal tasks as a share of total hours is falling relatively slower.

Box 2: Estimating Task Shifts

For this analysis, the report uses what the literature refers to as a "task-based" approach. It starts by identifying the employment breakdown of the industry according to occupations using labor force survey data. This provides an overview of the occupations in an industry and the relative employment by occupation for 43 occupations, aggregated into five major groups: managerial; technical (e.g., analyst, engineer); administrative (e.g., secretary); customer-facing; manual (e.g., floor workers).

For each of the occupations in the industry, a "task profile" was developed. A task profile gives a detailed description of the average number of hours per week a worker spends executing specific tasks. Based on the literature, the five different task groups listed above were identified.[a] To create individual task profiles for each of the occupations in the relevant industries, data collected by the World Bank's Skills Measurement Program (STEP) were used.[b] Questions from the survey allocated time spent on task groups. The amount of time spent on routine versus nonroutine tasks was determined, then each time allocation was further split between physical, interpersonal, and analytical tasks. The result is a profile of the relative time, in terms of hours spent, of each the five task groups for each occupation in the industry.

To understand how these task profiles shift with Industry 4.0 (4IR) technology adoption, estimates from the employer survey were used. Employers were asked to estimate the change in aggregate time spent by task in their firm (i.e., change in the total time all workers in the firm spend on the set task collectively) due to 4IR technology adoption over the next 5 years. The fundamental assumption is that the adoption of 4IR technologies changes the task profile of an occupation through automation of certain tasks and time shifted to others. This results in new task profiles by occupation for 2030 where 100% of firms have adopted 4IR.

[a] Prospera and AlphaBeta Advisors. 2019. *Capturing Indonesia's Automation Potential.* https://www.alphabeta.com/wp-content/uploads/2019/08/capturing-indonesias-automation-potential.pdf.

[b] World Bank. The STEP Skills Measurement Program. https://microdata.worldbank.org/index.php/catalog/step/about.

Source: Asian Development Bank and AlphaBeta.

Skills Implications

These task shifts will potentially have significant implications for the aggregate skills required in the industry. The analysis considers 10 categories of skills:[20]

(i)   **Critical thinking and adaptive learning.** Skills that allow using logic and reasoning to identify the strengths and weaknesses of alternative solutions, conclusions or approaches to problems as well as understanding the implications of new information for both current and future problem-solving and decision-making.

(ii)   **Written and verbal communication.** Ability to read, write, speak, and actively listen.

(iii)   **Numeracy.** Ability to use mathematics, and scientific rules and methods to solve problems.

(iv)   **Complex problem solving.** Skills that help identify complex problems and review related information to develop and evaluate options and implement solutions.

(v)   **Management.** Skills that help allocate financial, material, personnel, and time resources efficiently.

---

[20]   The 10 skill categories and their definitions were chosen to align with the six skill groups provided by O*NET, which is one of the key databases for examining skill changes in the workforce. Some adjustments were made to the O*NET classifications to better align with the analysis. These included disaggregating O*NET's Basic Skill group into critical thinking and adaptive learning, written and verbal communication, and numeracy; and computer literacy and digital/information and communication technology skills being broken out of O*NETs broader Technical Skill group due to their particular relevance for 4IR.

Figure 6: Employers' Expected Impact of 4IR on Working Time Spent on Different Tasks in Viet Nam's Logistics Industry, 2018–2025

Logistics: Tasks

Rather than jobs, the majority of the impact is likely to be on tasks,
with physical tasks and routine interpersonal tasks likely to see strong decline

Percent of survey respondents (%)

Legend: Decrease >20%, Decrease 0%-20%, No change, Increase 0%-20%, Increase >20%

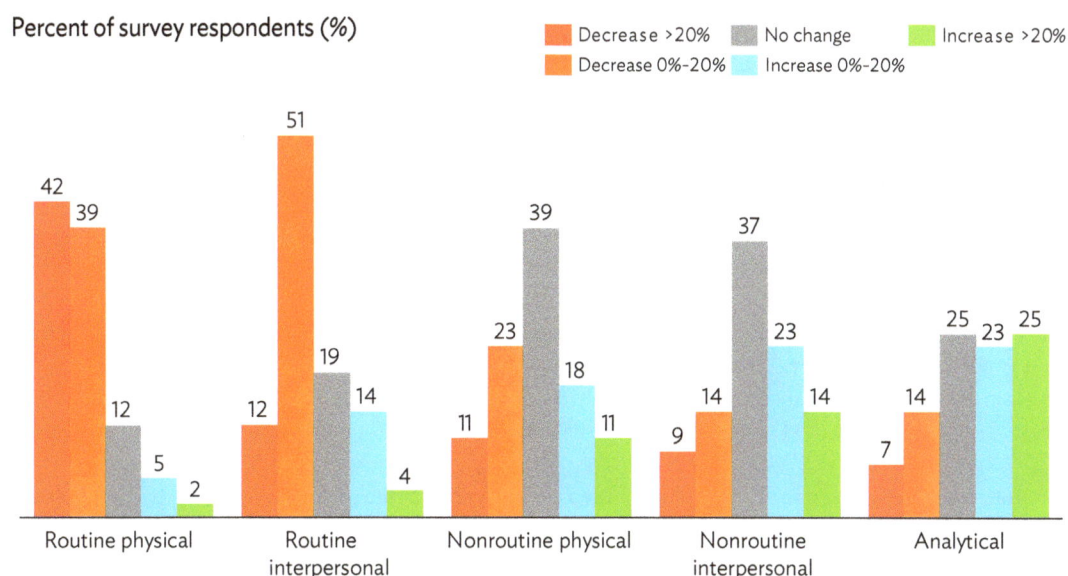

4IR = Industry 4.0 or Fourth Industrial Revolution.

Note: Answers in the chart do not sum to 100% as figure for the response "Don't know" was not included.

Sources: Employer survey on impact of 4IR on the logistics industry in Viet Nam, n=57.

(vi) **Social.** Skills that help to work with people to achieve goals such as coordination, instructing, negotiation, persuasion, service orientation and social perceptiveness/empathy.

(vii) **Evaluation, judgment, and decision-making.** Skills used to understand, monitor, conduct and improve analysis and socio-technical systems.

(viii) **Technical.** Skills used to design, set-up, operate, maintain, and correct malfunctions involving application of machines or technological systems.

(ix) **Computer literacy.** Skills that allow workers to effectively use computers and digital applications in their jobs such as using email, word processing, searching the internet, data entry etc.

(x) **Digital/information and communication technology.** Skills that allow workers to work in inherently digital occupations and perform complex tasks in a digital environment, as well as operating and/or developing digital tools such as advanced spreadsheet functions, financial software, graphical design, statistical analysis, software programming or managing computer networks.

Box 3: Estimating Skills Changes

To compute "current skill profiles" for each occupation in the industry, data from the World Bank's Skills Measurement Program (STEP) questionnaire's "Module 6: Work Skills" were used. Questions from this chapter were used to assess the importance of each skill category. A value from a scale of 0–3 (0 for "skill is not used" to 3, "highly advanced skills are required") was assigned to skills based on survey responses to relevant questions. The score measures both the importance as well the competency level of the skill for each skill category.

Future skill profiles leveraged two sources of data: (i) data on skill and education requirements from job profiles for occupations, obtained from online job portals; and (ii) information about changes in skill requirements from the employer survey.

The collected job postings were analyzed in detail and assigned an importance/skill competency score (from 0–3) for each of the 10 skill categories. They were also categorized according to the five job groups identified above: managerial, administrative, technical, customer-facing, and manual.

In parallel, as a second estimate, employer survey data were leveraged to understand which skill categories would gain in importance due to adoption of Industry 4.0 at an industry level. Based on the responses, percentage changes in the level of importance scores were calculated for the five job groups. Applying these to the current skill profiles based on STEP resulted in a second set of estimates for future skills profiles.

The future skills profiles used to estimate the skills gap were then computed as an average of the two estimates and the skill gap by occupation was identified by simply examining the differences in importance scores between current and future skill profiles.

Source: World Bank. 2019. The STEP Skills Measurement Program. https://microdata.worldbank.org/index.php/catalog/step.

Box 3 describes the approach used to understand the potential impacts on 4IR on the skills required by workers.

Based on the skills categories, unique, current, and future (i.e., post-4IR technology adoption) skill profiles for occupations in the industry were computed based on data from the World Bank STEP survey, job portal data, as well as inputs from the employer survey. These profiles were then compared to understand the skills gap created by 4IR technology adoption.

The analysis highlights some significant changes in the skill requirements in the industry:

(i)   **Change in skills demand.** This study reviewed both employer survey data as well as job portal data to understand changes in the importance of skills linked to 4IR. Interestingly, while employers perceived digital and computer literacy skills to be the fastest increasing skill categories, the job portal data reflected these to be critical thinking and complex problem-solving skills (Figure 7).

Figure 7: Potential Impact of 4IR on Shifts in the Importance of Different Skills in Viet Nam's Logistics Industry

Logistics: Skills

While employers believe that digital and ICT skills will rise most in importance, job portal data reflect this to be critical thinking

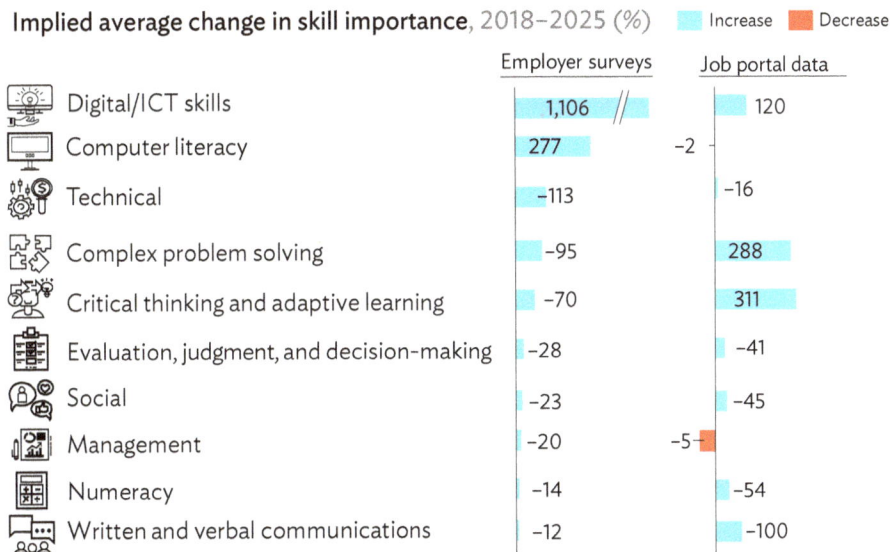

Implied average change in skill importance, 2018–2025 (%)   ▪ Increase   ▪ Decrease

	Employer surveys	Job portal data
Digital/ICT skills	1,106 //	120
Computer literacy	277	−2
Technical	−113	−16
Complex problem solving	−95	288
Critical thinking and adaptive learning	−70	311
Evaluation, judgment, and decision-making	−28	−41
Social	−23	−45
Management	−20	−5
Numeracy	−14	−54
Written and verbal communications	−12	−100

4IR = Industry 4.0 or Fourth Industrial Revolution, GDP = gross domestic product, GSO = General Statistics Office (Viet Nam), ICT = information and communication technology, ILO = International Labour Organization, IMF = International Monetary Fund, LFS = Labour Force Surveys (Viet Nam), STEP = Systematic Tracking of Exchanges in Procurement.

Sources: Industry employment – GSO, LFS 2017 and ILO; GDP/Output – GSO and IMF Article IV; STEP survey data; Employer survey on impact of 4IR on the logistics industry in Viet Nam, n= 57+; Job portal data: jobs in the logistics industry scraped from the job portal VietnamWorks over the period from July to August 2019.

(ii) **Overall skill importance.** Evaluation, judgment, and decision-making; social; numeracy; verbal and written communication; and critical thinking are all likely to see their relative importance increase by 2030 (Figure 8). Management is forecast to see the greatest relative decline in skills importance as delivery scheduling and routing will increasingly be done by algorithms.

(iii) **Changes in level of skills.** Overall, the industry will require significant upskilling as the demand for more intermediate and advanced skills is likely to increase (Figure 9). In particular, the industry will require an increase in the number of workers with intermediate critical thinking and written and verbal communication as well as advanced evaluation and social skills. While their relative importance in the industry is likely to remain low, many workers will require basic computer literacy and digital skills.

Figure 8: Impact of 4IR on the Importance of Different Skills in Viet Nam's Logistics Industry, 2018–2030

Logistics: Skills

4IR adoption could cause evaluation, decision-making, and social skills to be most important, while management skills could see a decline

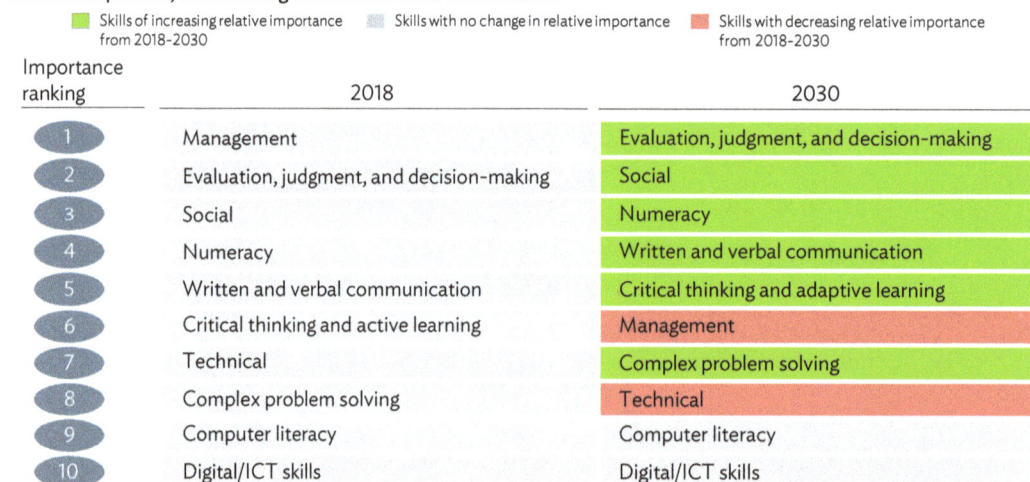

■ Skills of increasing relative importance from 2018-2030   ■ Skills with no change in relative importance   ■ Skills with decreasing relative importance from 2018-2030

Importance ranking	2018	2030
1	Management	Evaluation, judgment, and decision-making
2	Evaluation, judgment, and decision-making	Social
3	Social	Numeracy
4	Numeracy	Written and verbal communication
5	Written and verbal communication	Critical thinking and adaptive learning
6	Critical thinking and active learning	Management
7	Technical	Complex problem solving
8	Complex problem solving	Technical
9	Computer literacy	Computer literacy
10	Digital/ICT skills	Digital/ICT skills

4IR = Industry 4.0 or Fourth Industrial Revolution, GDP = gross domestic product, GSO = General Statistics Office (Viet Nam), ICT = information and communication technology, ILO = International Labour Organization, IMF = International Monetary Fund, LFS = Labour Force Surveys (Viet Nam), STEP = Systematic Tracking of Exchanges in Procurement.
Source: Industry employment – GSO, LFS 2017 and ILO; GDP/Output – GSO and IMF Article IV; STEP survey data; Employer survey on impact of 4IR on the logistics industry in Viet Nam, n= 57+; Job portal data: jobs in the logistics industry scraped from the job portal VietnamWorks over the period from July to August 2019.

Figure 9: Absolute Change in Percentage of Workers Requiring Skills, 2018–2030
(%)

Logistics: Skills

4IR adoption will require large increases in intermediate critical thinking and communication, as well as advance social and evaluation skills

Skills	Basic	Intermediate	Advanced
Critical thinking and adaptive learning	−72.7	77.3	10.5
Written and verbal communication	−79.2	75.9	3.4
Numeracy	−15.8	3.2	12.6
Complex problem solving	4.5	78.4	7.4
Management	−0.1	0.1	0.0
Social	−14.3	−71.7	86.0
Evaluation, judgment, and decision-making	−0.1	−99.8	99.9
Technical	−53.8	77.4	2.3
Computer literacy	84.3	1.9	4.4
Digital/ICT skills	84.5	7.9	1.0

Legend: ■ >50 ■ >10 ■ ≤10; ≥−10 ■ <−10 ■ < −50

4IR = Industry 4.0 or Fourth Industrial Revolution, GDP = gross domestic product, GSO = General Statistics Office (Viet Nam), ICT = information and communication technology, ILO = International Labour Organization, IMF = International Monetary Fund, LFS = Labour Force Surveys (Viet Nam), STEP = Systematic Tracking of Exchanges in Procurement.
Sources: Industry employment – GSO, LFS 2017 and ILO; GDP/Output – GSO and IMF Article IV; STEP survey data; Employer survey on impact of 4IR on the logistics industry in Viet Nam, n= 57+; Job portal data: jobs in the logistics industry scraped from the job portal VietnamWorks over the period from July to August 2019.

Box 4: Comparison of Insights in the Logistics Industry Versus Past Research

The logistics industry in Viet Nam, and in particular its workforce, have been the subject of many recent studies. While few studies have looked at the direct employment and skill-related impacts of Industry 4.0 (4IR), many have tried to understand the general labor trends in the industry. For example, research by the Viet Nam Logistics Research and Development Institute (VLI) and Viet Nam Logistics Business Association (VLA) surveyed business on their logistics hiring trends.[a] VLI research projected that 200,000 professional logistics employees or workers (akin to what this research refers to as managerial, technical, administrative and customer facing occupations) will be required by 2030. This result is in line with the predictions of this research, which estimates the number of additional jobs by 2030 at approximately 210,000 workers. However, this addition is purely driven by 4IR technology adoption and does not account for other external factors such as increases in the international competitiveness of Viet Nam's logistic sector, which would undoubtedly lead to additional demand.

On the skills front, research by the World Bank identified a list of key skills that were currently lacking in the logistics industry by different types of workers, i.e., operative, administrative, supervisory, and managerial. These included: basic and specific logistics skills, basic calculation, computer literacy, English skills, soft skills such as discipline, time management, compliance (e.g., not accepting informal payments), team work, problem solving, communications and customer relationship skills.[b]

According to the VLA/VLI research, communication and negotiation skills, professional and/or technical skills, and English language proficiency were given more weight in hiring decisions. Numeracy skills were also highlighted as important. Communication and social skills (critical for negotiation) are also among those found to be of increasing importance in this research; however, the predictions in this report suggest that while technical skills will increase in importance, they will do so at a slower rate than other skill categories over the next 10 years. The assessment of staff competencies undertaken as part of the VLA/VLI research places the ability to work independently as the highest scoring skill in the industry, which is consistent with the finding in this research that management (including self- and time management) skills are of greatest importance in the industry today. However, this research suggests that management skills may become of lesser importance relative to other skill categories over the next 10 years.

[a] AusAid, VLA, VLI. 2019. *Brief Report on the Current Status of the Logistics Workforce in Viet Nam.*
[b] World Bank. 2019. *Viet Nam: Assessment of Logistics Skills, Training, and Competencies of Male and Female Employees.*
Source: Asian Development Bank and AlphaBeta.

Skills Supply Trends

Figure 10 shows the breakdown of the additional demand for training that will be required by workers in the logistics industry under 4IR technology adoption. This reflects the volume of training required to bring the logistics workforce in Viet Nam from the skills required in 2018, to the level of skills required by 2030, driven only by 4IR technology adoption. Figure 10 shows that most of the training requirements will likely come from on-the-job training, since many of the skill improvements either require marginal increases in skill level that do not warrant formal training or education, or the workers requiring it will continue to be in employment but need to adjust to a new way of working (i.e., new skill profiles) under 4IR. This resonates with earlier research by the Viet Nam Logistics Research and Development Institute (VLI) and Viet Nam Logistics Business Association (VLA), where a survey of logistics businesses found that there was increasing focus on holding internal trainings and sending staff to short-term trainings provided by other entities.[21]

21   AusAid, VLA, VLI. 2019. *Brief Report on the Current Status of the Logistics Workforce in Viet Nam.*

Figure 10: Additional Person Trainings Required to Meet Skills Demand Driven by 4IR in 2030 In Viet Nam's Logistics Industry, by Type of Training

Logistics: Skills

65% of the additional demand for training driven by Industry 4.0 adoption
will likely need to be met by on-the-job training

Millions of person trainings required by type of training

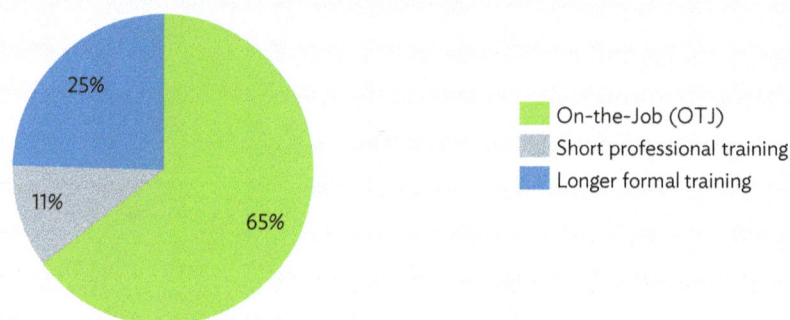

- 25%
- 11%
- 65%

Legend:
- On-the-Job (OTJ)
- Short professional training
- Longer formal training

4IR = Industry 4.0 or Fourth Industrial Revolution.
Notes:
1. Figures include rounding adjustments.
2. One person training refers to training one worker, in one skill from the level required by his occupation's skill profile in 2018 to the relevant level given by the skills profile in 2030.
3. "On-the-job" training refers to training conducted during day to day such as senior staff instructing junior staff or running internal seminars; "Short professional" training refers to short (from 1 day to 6 months) courses conducted by professional internal or external instructors (e.g., weekend seminars, boot-camps). "Longer formal" trainings refer to trainings longer than 6 months for which workers would likely have to take leave from their jobs, these include returning into formal education such as obtaining a degree.
Sources: Industry employment – GSO, LFS 2017 and ILO; GDP/Output – GSO and IMF Article IV; STEP survey data; Employer survey on impact of 4IR on the logistics industry in Viet Nam, n= 57+; Job portal data: jobs in the logistics industry scraped from the job portal VietnamWorks over the period from July to August 2019.

To better understand the training and education sector, in Viet Nam two surveys were conducted. As part of the survey of employers in the logistics industry, respondents were asked to comment on their ability to attract good candidates for jobs as well as their current engagement in training efforts. Further, a separate training institute survey was commissioned, the results of which are discussed in Chapter 2.

Survey results of employers in the logistics industry reveal that while the majority of employers feel that there are sufficient graduates to meet their company's entry-level hiring needs, less than 50% of employers find it easy to identify high-quality graduates and only 37% agreed (or strongly agreed) that graduates hired in the last year had been adequately prepared by their previous education or training (Figure 11). This is in line with findings by the Viet Nam Trade Facilitation and Competitiveness Program of the Australia-World Bank Group Strategic Partnership in Viet Nam, whose employer interviews in the logistics industry concluded that the availability of logistics education by private training providers was found lacking.[22]

---

[22] World Bank. 2019. *Viet Nam: Assessment of Logistics Skills, Training, and Competencies of Male and Female Employees.*

Box 5: Estimating Training Requirements

Skills supply, i.e., training requirements, can be quantified in person training. One-person training refers to training one worker, in one skill from the level specified by the person's occupation profile in the industry, in 2018, to the required level under Industry 4.0 (4IR) technology adoption. Hence, the training required to shift a worker from the worker's current skill profile to the future one would require one-person training per skill that needs improvement between 2018 and 2030.

To understand the type of training needed, in particular, the length of training, two factors need to be considered: (i) understanding the level of skill improvement needed, and (ii) understanding the access to different training channels by different workers.

Individuals' training needs are going to differ if they require an improvement of skills from basic to intermediate levels, intermediate to advanced levels, or even basic to advanced levels. For example, a worker who only requires basic technical skills today, but requires advanced technical skills in 2030 under 4IR technology adoption, will likely require more training than another worker who only has to improve skills from intermediate to advanced. This also goes for workers who do not need a particular skill today, but will require it in 2030, whether basic, intermediate, or advanced.

Apart from the length of training required to obtain a certain level of skills, the access to different channels of training may not be the same for all workers in the industry. For example, workers displaced from their jobs may not be able to receive on-the-job training, but require formal training prior to being able to find new employment. Similarly, for future generations of workers (i.e., students currently in formal education or training), it may make more sense to embed skill training in their formal curriculum, rather than waiting to train them on-the-job. Three categories of workers impacted by 4IR were identified based on the skill demand analysis:

(i) **Workers in need of reskilling.** These workers will likely lose their current jobs due to automation, meaning they need to receive training that makes them employable in new jobs created.
(ii) **Workers in need of upskilling.** These workers will likely remain in their occupations, but the adoption of 4IR technologies means they will have to acquire new skills as well as advance existing skills to upgrade to their future skill profile.
(iii) **Future workers.** These will be additional workers required to fill the jobs generated from growing demand. Hence, they are workers that did not previously work in the industry, but could either join as new graduates or professional hires from other industries.

The distinction of the type of worker is important as different workers have access to different types of training. For example, while future workers are likely to receive some of their skill training in the formal education industry, returning to formal education is an unlikely option for workers in need of upskilling, who will continue to be employed during their training.

Source: Asian Development Bank and AlphaBeta.

Figure 11: Employer Sentiment Toward Graduates Hired in the Past 24 Months

Logistics: Skills

While there seem to be enough graduates to fill positions in the industry, the education and training they have received may not be sufficient

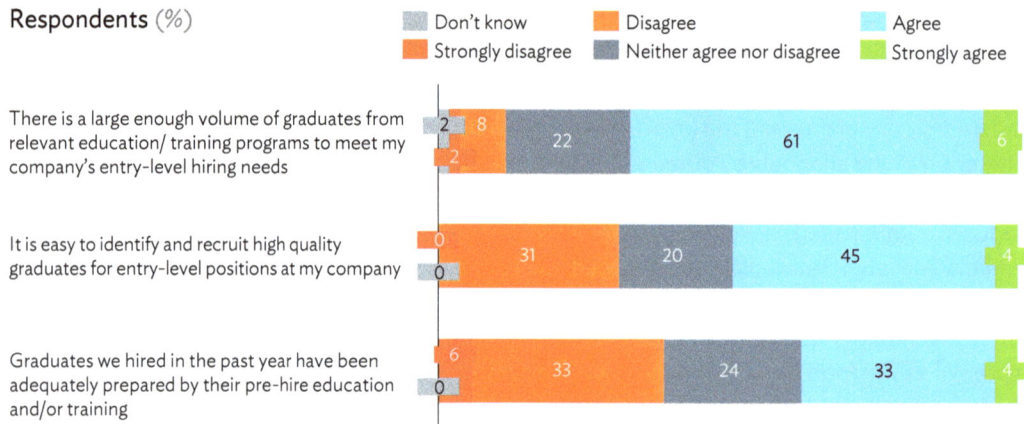

Respondents (%)

Legend: Don't know | Disagree | Agree | Strongly disagree | Neither agree nor disagree | Strongly agree

There is a large enough volume of graduates from relevant education/ training programs to meet my company's entry-level hiring needs
2 | 8 | 2 | 22 | 61 | 6

It is easy to identify and recruit high quality graduates for entry-level positions at my company
0 | 31 | 0 | 20 | 45 | 4

Graduates we hired in the past year have been adequately prepared by their pre-hire education and/or training
6 | 33 | 0 | 24 | 33 | 4

Sources: Employer survey on impact of Industry 4.0 on the logistics industry in Viet Nam, n=51.

Agro-processing Industry

The impact of 4IR could be significant in agro-processing, but employer surveys in Viet Nam suggest there is limited understanding of the potential benefits. McKinsey has estimated that labor productivity could improve by around 50% in the food sector through adoption of 4IR technologies.[23] However, there is no clear consensus on potential productivity benefits from the survey of Vietnamese firms in the agro-processing sector. The displacement of jobs could be significant, with a third of jobs in the current workforce at risk of automation (versus 26% in the logistics sector). The challenge will be to redirect these workers into new occupations, as well as provide them with the right skills to continue to stay in their occupations in a 4IR-dominated landscape. To achieve this, a significant amount of additional training between 2018 and 2030 will be required, and in addition to on-the-job training, there will be a significant amount of longer formal training required to bridge some significant skill gaps in the industry.

23 Arbulu, I. et al. 2018. *Industry 4.0: Reinvigorating ASEAN Manufacturing for the Future.* McKinsey & Company. 8 February. https://www.mckinsey.com/business-functions/operations/our-insights/industry-4-0-reinvigorating-asean-manufacturing-for-the-future.

Relevance to Industry 4.0

Previous research has identified a range of technologies that could transform every aspect of the agro-processing value chain, ranging from the adoption of big data to improve decision-making to using IoT technologies to track products.[24]

Some key technologies include:

(i) **Rethinking production approaches through digital innovations**. Process monitoring and control can be automated on the factory floor utilizing a combination of IoT, cloud computing, and AI. This can enable machines to monitor and analyze manufacturing processes, detect any deviations, and implement necessary adjustments without human intervention. Improvements in technologies such as digital image processing can also enable more accurate food quality inspection, including verification of labeling accuracy, colors, and height or volume.[25] Redesign of manufacturing processes can also leverage virtual reality or augmented reality devices, which can simulate different manufacturing designs in an immersive manner.

(ii) **Use of robotics on the production floor.** Food processing has historically proved challenging for the use of robotics due to the high volumes, with variable shapes and sizes. This can create a challenge for when robots try to grasp an item, particularly if it is delicate (as is the case for many food items). Advancements have now seen robots with "soft grippers" that can quickly but gently handle sensitive food products, such as fruits and vegetables. Other types of grippers, such as vacuum grippers, are increasingly able to handle delicate or irregularly shaped items, particularly when coupled with imaging technology.[26]

(iii) **Utilization of biotech to support the development of alternative proteins.** Currently, the market size of alternative proteins is approximately $2.2 billion compared with a global meat market of approximately $1.7 trillion, but it is growing rapidly, driven by a combination of environmental and health concerns.[27] There are a range of opportunities in agro-processing linked to the development of alternative proteins, including plant proteins, microbial proteins, and cultured meat. This requires using a range of technologies, including big data approaches for protein identification and the development of biotech-based methods for high-value, sustainable, and nutritious protein production.[28]

(iv) **Tackling food waste through biotech.** Globally, about 30% of all food that is produced is wasted, representing $1 trillion in lost economic value annually (footnote 28). Biotech technologies such as irradiation can help reduce post-harvest losses through disinfestations, sprout inhibition, and improving the shelf-life of fresh produce. It can also be effective in reducing food-borne diseases through the destruction of pathogens.

---

[24] Food Innovation Australia Limited. 2017. Size of the Prize: An Overview of 16 Opportunities for Australian Food & Agribusinesses. https://fial.com.au/size-of-the-prize-report.

[25] N. Z. N. Hasnan and Y. Yusoff. 2018. Application Areas of Industry 4.0 Technologies in Food Processing Sector. https://www.semanticscholar.org/paper/Short-review%3A-Application-Areas-of-Industry-4.0-in-Hasnan-Yusoff/702d5dab564c1d3 2f012642dc4ce3dc0955a5b50.

[26] Robotics Industry Association. 2019. Robotics in Food Manufacturing and Food Processing. https://www.robotics.org/blog-articlecfm/Robotics-in-Food-Manufacturing-and-Food-Processing/154.

[27] Z. Bashi et al. 2019. Alternative Proteins: The Race for Market Share Is On. *McKinsey & Company*. 16 August. https://www.mckinsey.com/industries/agriculture/our-insights/alternative-proteins-the-race-for-market-share-is-on.

[28] FAO. 2019. *State of Food and Agriculture 2019: Moving Forward On Food Loss And Waste Reduction*. http://www.fao.org/3/ca6030en/ca6030en.pdf.

(v) **Customized food development through 3D printing.** In response to the desire to meet customer's personalized needs, there is increasing use of 3D printing in food processing. This is where the ingredients are deposited by layers in a sequential process according to the recipe, configured shape and layout. Advancements in 3D printing are seeing the application of edible cement as binding materials. While still nascent in their use in food processing, 3D printers could have applications due to the ability to develop intricate designs, customizable product offerings, and minimize wastage (footnote 25). Given the speed of development of additive manufacturing or 3D printing, there could be a point where it becomes cost effective for households to own these, which could create a significant disruption to the food processing sector.

(vi) **Internet of Things to manage supply chains.** IoT refers to networks of sensors and actuators embedded in machines and other physical objects that connect with one another and the Internet. It has a wide range of applications, including data collection, monitoring, decision-making, and process optimization.[29] RFID tags on containers can track products as they move from the factory to stores, allowing companies to avoid stock-outs and losses. Tighter management of supply chains can help to significantly minimize food waste, and also improve product traceability to enhance food safety and reduce food fraud.

Of the agro-processing employers surveyed in Viet Nam, 40% claim to have already adopted 4IR technologies. However, 68% stated that costs are a significant barrier to implementation (Figure 12).[30]

It appears from the survey data that most employers in the agro-processing industry in Viet Nam are unclear about the productivity improvements their industry can expect from 4IR over the next 5 years (Figure 13). Of the surveyed employers, 37% admit that they simply do not know, whereas the remaining are evenly split across different productivity estimates.

Despite this, many businesses have plans to adopt 4IR; for example, in food processing, 25% of businesses are planning to engage in medium- to large-scale adoption over the next 5 years (footnote 4).

---

[29] J. Woetzl et al. 2014. *Southeast Asia at the Crossroads: Three Paths to Prosperity.* McKinsey Global Institute. November. https://www.mckinsey.com/~/media/McKinsey/Featured%20Insights/Asia%20Pacific/Three%20paths%20to%20sustained%20economic%20growth%20in%20Southeast%20Asia/MGI%20SE%20Asia_Executive%20summary_November%202014.ashx.

[30] Based on 71 completed responses.

Figure 12: Sentiments Toward 4IR in the Agro-Processing Industry in Viet Nam

Agro-processing: 4IR readiness

Companies in the agro-processing industry claim to have a good understanding of 4IR technologies but almost 70% see cost as a barrier

Respondents (%)

Legend: Don't know | Disagree | Agree | Strongly disagree | Neither agree nor disagree | Strongly agree

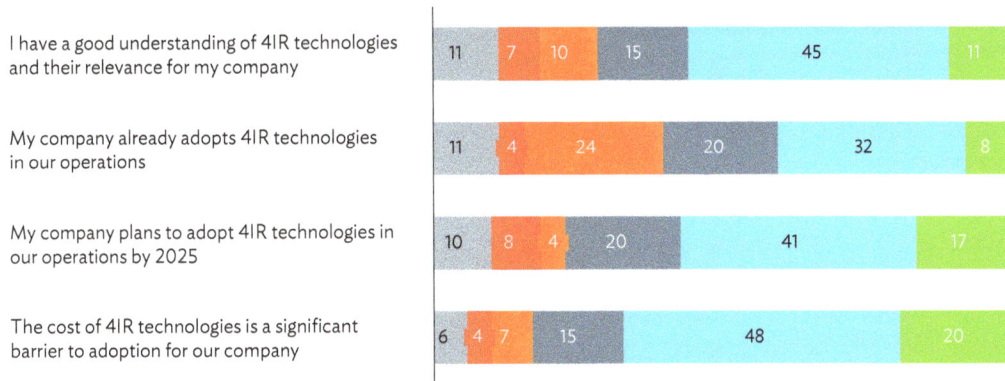

Statement	Don't know	Strongly disagree	Disagree	Neither agree nor disagree	Agree	Strongly agree
I have a good understanding of 4IR technologies and their relevance for my company	11	7	10	15	45	11
My company already adopts 4IR technologies in our operations	11	4	24	20	32	8
My company plans to adopt 4IR technologies in our operations by 2025	10	8	4	20	41	17
The cost of 4IR technologies is a significant barrier to adoption for our company	6	4	7	15	48	20

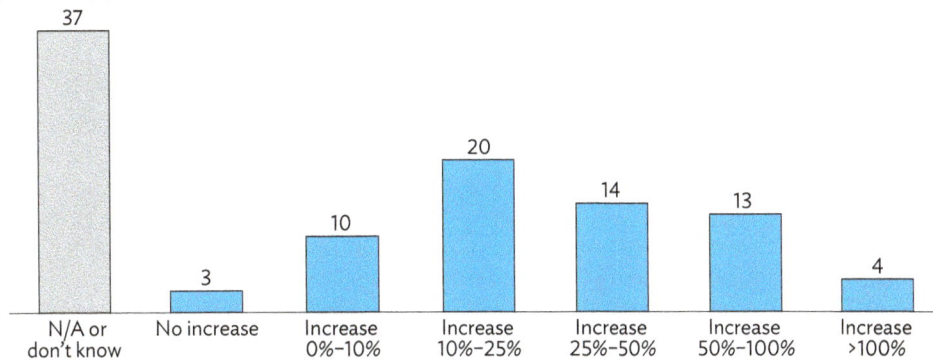

4IR = Industry 4.0 or Fourth Industrial Revolution.
Sources: Employer survey on impact of 4IR on the agro-processing industry in Viet Nam, n=71.

Figure 13: Expected Productivity Improvement Due to 4IR Technologies in 5 Years

Agro-processing: Jobs

There is little consensus among employers in the agro-processing industry on the likely productivity increase from 4IR over the next 5 years

Respondents (%)

Category	%
N/A or don't know	37
No increase	3
Increase 0%–10%	10
Increase 10%–25%	20
Increase 25%–50%	14
Increase 50%–100%	13
Increase >100%	4

4IR = Industry 4.0 or Fourth Industrial Revolution.
Source: Employer survey on impact of 4IR on the agro-processing industry in Viet Nam, n=71.

Skills Demand Analysis

Employment Implications

Similar to what was observed in the logistics industry, the analysis predicts a net positive impact on total employment for the agro-processing industry in 2030 from 4IR technology adoption (Figure 14). However, the magnitude of the displacement and the income effect are much greater than what is observed in logistics. Due to the huge potential productivity benefits in this industry (up to 50% according to McKinsey), the potential income effect is significant (potentially growing jobs by 68% from today's levels), while the displacement effect stems mostly from the significant risk of automation of processing and machine operator roles (footnote 23).

As with the logistics industry, given the same challenges to realizing the positive income effect, Viet Nam's approach to skill development will be critical in realizing a positive labor-market outcome related to 4IR in this sector. Only suitable skills in the local workforce will allow displaced workers to be able to seamlessly move into newly created jobs.

Figure 14: Impact of 4IR on Number of Jobs in Viet Nam's Agro-Processing Industry, 2018–2030

Agro-processing: Jobs

The overall impact of 4IR on jobs is likely to be small and marginally positive as displacement is potentially offset by income effects

Displacement and income effects of 4IR on jobs, 2018-2030 (%)

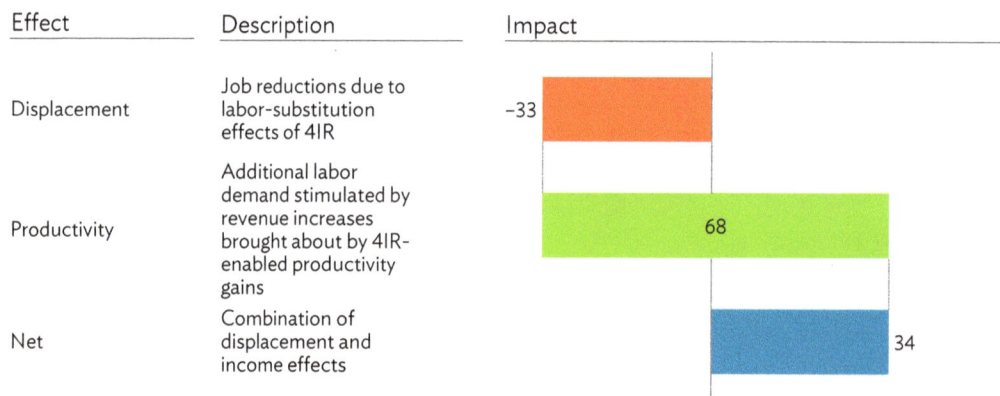

Effect	Description	Impact
Displacement	Job reductions due to labor-substitution effects of 4IR	−33
Productivity	Additional labor demand stimulated by revenue increases brought about by 4IR-enabled productivity gains	68
Net	Combination of displacement and income effects	34

4IR = Industry 4.0 or Fourth Industrial Revolution, GDP = gross domestic product, GSO = General Statistics Office (Viet Nam), ILO = International Labour Organization, IMF = International Monetary Fund, LFS = Labour Force Surveys (Viet Nam), STEP = Systematic Tracking of Exchanges in Procurement.

Note: Change in jobs based on accelerated adoption scenario of Industry 4.0 technologies.

Sources: Industry employment – GSO, LFS 2017 and ILO; GDP/Output – GSO, McKinsey and IMF Article IV; STEP survey data; Employer survey on impact of 4IR on the agro-processing industry in Viet Nam, n= 54+; Job portal data: jobs in the logistics industry scraped from the job portal VietnamWorks over the period from July to August 2019.

Another potential concern is that the displacement effect could adversely impact female workers. Agro-processing in Viet Nam is a predominantly female industry, with an over 2:1 female–to–male ratio. Further, some of the jobs at the highest risk of automation in this sector, such as food processing workers and machine operators, are currently female-dominated jobs. Overall, within the industry, 74% more women than men could be displaced by 4IR (Figure 15).

Job Task Implications

There are some interesting differences in the agro-processing industry compared to the logistics industry regarding the impact of 4IR on worker tasks. Routine interpersonal tasks are expected to see a slight increase in their share of worker time, with nonroutine skills and analytical tasks also likely to increase their share of total time in the average working week by 2030 (Figure 16). The decline in routine physical tasks is significantly more drastic for the agro-processing industry than in logistics, with a reduction of over a third of the time previously spent.

According to the results, workers in the industry could spend an additional 12.6% of their work week on interpersonal and other nonroutine tasks and 12.6% less on routine physical tasks (Figure 16).

Similar to the logistics industry, these results may seem surprising, as employers surveyed indicated that over the next 5 years they expect a decrease in time spent by 50% on routine interpersonal tasks and 41% on nonroutine physical tasks (Figure 17). However, given the large share of assembly line work in this sector (with high potential to be automated by 4IR technologies), it is perhaps not surprising that routine physical tasks are expected to decline so drastically, with time shifting to other tasks.

Figure 15: Displacement Effect of 4IR on Jobs Predominantly Held by Males Versus Females in Viet Nam's Agro-Processing Industry, 2018–2030

Agro-processing: Jobs

Displacement effects are projected to particularly impact manual as well as craft and related jobs, predominantly held by women

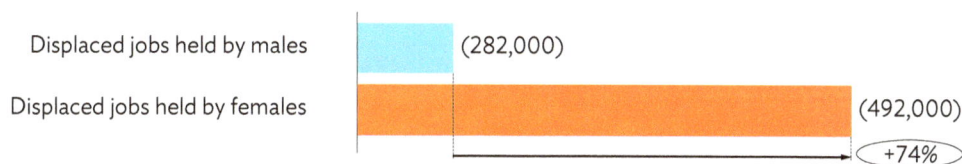

Displaced jobs held by males (282,000)

Displaced jobs held by females (492,000) +74%

4IR = Industry 4.0 or Fourth Industrial Revolution, GDP = gross domestic product, GSO = General Statistics Office (Viet Nam), ILO = International Labour Organization, IMF = International Monetary Fund, LFS = Labour Force Surveys (Viet Nam), STEP = Systematic Tracking of Exchanges in Procurement.

Source: Industry employment – GSO, LFS 2017 and ILO; GDP/Output – GSO, McKinsey and IMF Article IV; STEP survey data; Employer survey on impact of 4IR on the agro-processing industry in Viet Nam, n= 54+; Job portal data: jobs in the logistics industry scraped from the job portal VietnamWorks over the period from July to August 2019.

Figure 16: Shifts in Time Spent by Workers on Different Types of Tasks at Work in Viet Nam's Agro-Processing Industry, 2018–2030

Agro-processing: Tasks

4IR application in the agro-processing industry could potentially lead to a substantial reduction in the time spent on routine physical tasks

Average share of weekly working hours spent on this task (%)

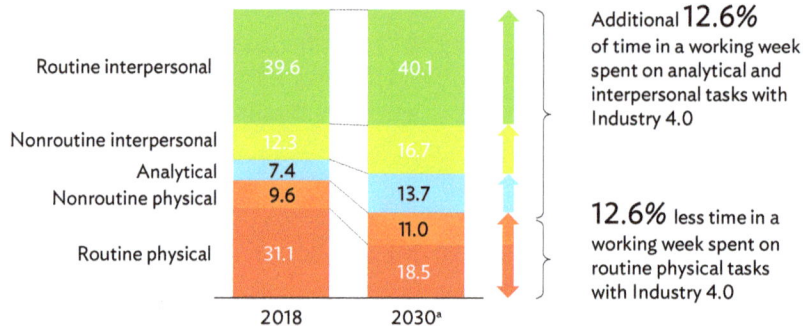

	2018	2030ᵃ
Routine interpersonal	39.6	40.1
Nonroutine interpersonal	12.3	16.7
Analytical	7.4	13.7
Nonroutine physical	9.6	11.0
Routine physical	31.1	18.5

Additional **12.6%** of time in a working week spent on analytical and interpersonal tasks with Industry 4.0

12.6% less time in a working week spent on routine physical tasks with Industry 4.0

4IR = Industry 4.0 or Fourth Industrial Revolution, GDP = gross domestic product, GSO = General Statistics Office (Viet Nam), ILO = International Labour Organization, IMF = International Monetary Fund, LFS = Labour Force Surveys (Viet Nam), STEP = Systematic Tracking of Exchanges in Procurement.

Note: Figures include rounding adjustments.

ᵃ Based on "high adoption" scenario of 4IR, the Appendix has more details.

Sources: Industry employment – GSO, LFS 2017 and ILO; GDP/Output – GSO, McKinsey and IMF Article IV; STEP survey data; Employer survey on impact of 4IR on the agro-processing industry in Viet Nam, n= 54+; Job portal data: jobs in the logistics industry scraped from the job portal VietnamWorks over the period from July to August 2019.

Figure 17: Employers' Expected Impact of 4IR on Working Time Spent on Different Tasks in Viet Nam's Agro-Processing Industry, 2018–2030

Agro-processing: Tasks

Rather than jobs, the majority of the impact is likely to be on tasks, with analytical tasks likely to rise while physical tasks decline

Percent of survey respondents (%)

Legend: Decrease >20% | Decrease 0%–20% | No change | Increase 0%–20% | Increase >20%

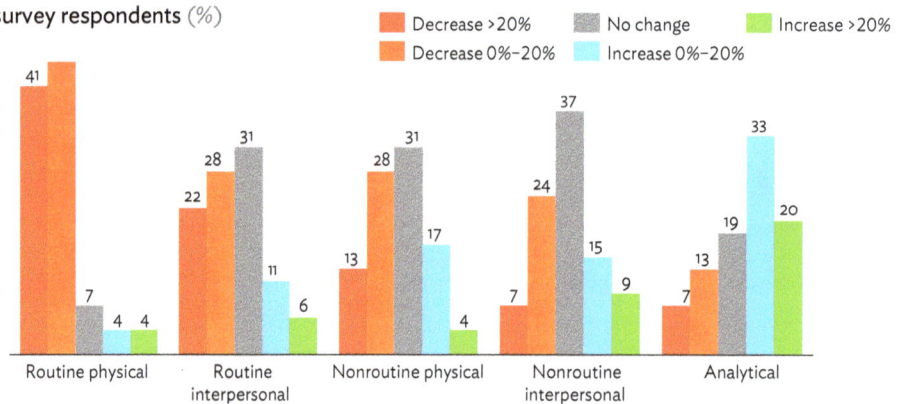

	Decrease >20%	Decrease 0%–20%	No change	Increase 0%–20%	Increase >20%
Routine physical	41	7	4	4	
Routine interpersonal	22	28	31	11	6
Nonroutine physical	13	28	31	17	4
Nonroutine interpersonal	7	24	37	15	9
Analytical	7	13	19	33	20

4IR = Industry 4.0 or Fourth Industrial Revolution.

Note: Answers in above chart do not sum to 100% as figure for the response "Don't know" was not included.

Source: Employer survey on impact of 4IR on the agro-processing industry in Viet Nam, n=54.

Skills Implications

The analysis highlights some significant potential changes in the skill requirements in the industry:

(i) **Change in skills demand.** While the overall pattern in skill shift is similar to that in the logistics industry, the magnitude of the predicted changes varies in the agro-processing industry. For example, complex problem-solving skills are likely to be significantly more important than critical thinking for the agro-processing industry. The contrary is true in the logistics industry. Interestingly, there are some differences in the insights from the employer survey and online job board data (Figure 18). For example, complex problem solving is becoming much more important based on the online job portal data than based on the employer survey.

(ii) **Overall skill importance.** Evaluation, judgment, and decision-making; numeracy; and technical skills will likely be the most important skills by 2030 under full 4IR technology adoption (Figure 19). Technical skills in particular are estimated to have a large increase in relative importance, whereas management skills, as in the logistics industry, are forecast to see the greatest relative decline.

Figure 18: Potential Impact of 4IR on Shifts in the Importance of Different Skills in Viet Nam's Agro-Processing Industry

Agro-processing: Skills

Technical and ICT skills, problem solving and critical thinking are likely to become more important with 4IR

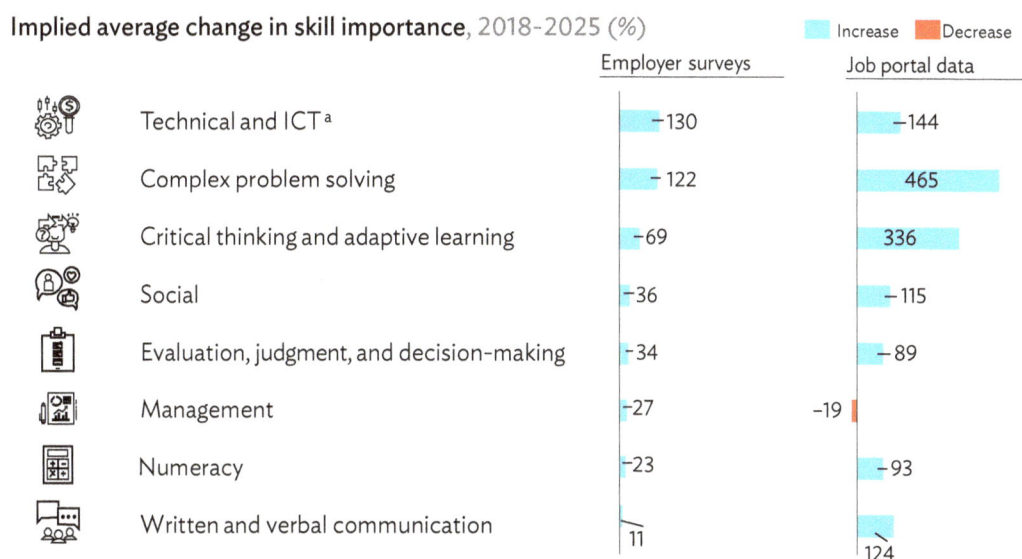

Implied average change in skill importance, 2018-2025 (%)

Increase Decrease

	Employer surveys	Job portal data
Technical and ICT [a]	−130	−144
Complex problem solving	−122	465
Critical thinking and adaptive learning	−69	336
Social	−36	−115
Evaluation, judgment, and decision-making	−34	−89
Management	−27	−19
Numeracy	−23	−93
Written and verbal communication	11	124

4IR = Industry 4.0 or Fourth Industrial Revolution, GDP = gross domestic product, GSO = General Statistics Office (Viet Nam), ICT = information and communication technology, ILO = International Labour Organization, IMF = International Monetary Fund, LFS = Labour Force Surveys (Viet Nam), STEP = Systematic Tracking of Exchanges in Procurement.

[a] For data from employer surveys and job portals to be comparable, "Technical," "Computer literacy," and "Digital/ICT" skills needed to be aggregated.

Sources: Industry employment – GSO, LFS 2017 and ILO; GDP/Output – GSO, McKinsey and IMF Article IV; STEP survey data; Employer survey on impact of 4IR on the agro-processing industry in Viet Nam, n= 54+; Job portal data: jobs in the logistics industry scraped from the job portal VietnamWorks over the period from July to August 2019.

Figure 19: Impact of 4IR on the Importance of Different Skills in Viet Nam's Agro-Processing Industry, 2018–2030

Agro-processing: Skills

4IR adoption is likely to lead to evaluation, numeracy, and technical skills becoming the most important skills in the agro-processing industry

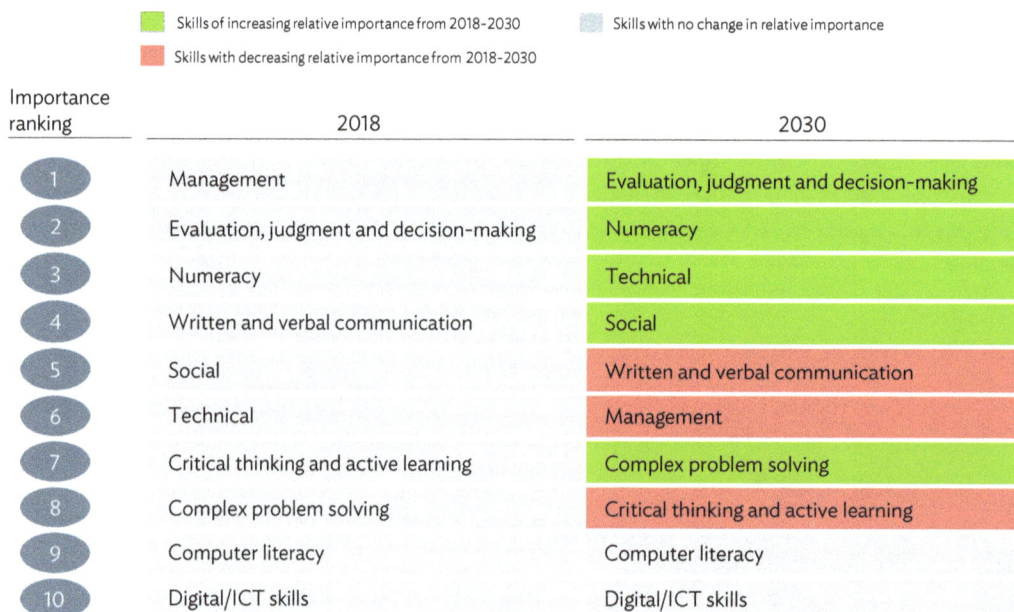

- Skills of increasing relative importance from 2018–2030
- Skills with decreasing relative importance from 2018–2030
- Skills with no change in relative importance

Importance ranking	2018	2030
1	Management	Evaluation, judgment and decision-making
2	Evaluation, judgment and decision-making	Numeracy
3	Numeracy	Technical
4	Written and verbal communication	Social
5	Social	Written and verbal communication
6	Technical	Management
7	Critical thinking and active learning	Complex problem solving
8	Complex problem solving	Critical thinking and active learning
9	Computer literacy	Computer literacy
10	Digital/ICT skills	Digital/ICT skills

4IR = Industry 4.0 or Fourth Industrial Revolution, GDP = gross domestic product, GSO = General Statistics Office (Viet Nam), ICT = information and communication technology, ILO = International Labour Organization, IMF = International Monetary Fund, LFS = Labour Force Surveys (Viet Nam), STEP = Systematic Tracking of Exchanges in Procurement.

Sources: Industry employment – GSO, LFS 2017 and ILO; GDP/Output – GSO, McKinsey and IMF Article IV; STEP survey data; Employer survey on impact of 4IR on the agro-processing industry in Viet Nam, n= 54+; Job portal data: jobs in the logistics industry scraped from the job portal VietnamWorks over the period from July to August 2019.

(iii)   **Changes in level of skills.** Overall, the industry will require significant upskilling as the demand for more intermediate and advanced skills is likely to increase (Figure 20). As opposed to the logistics industry, a greater demand for a wider range of advanced skills such as technical, computer literacy, and written and verbal communication skills is predicted. Interestingly, significantly more workers will require basic computer literacy skills, and some will require advanced skills, but the agro-processing industry might actually see a decrease in workers requiring intermediate computer literacy skills.

Figure 20: Impact of 4IR on the Level of Skills Required in Viet Nam's Logistics Industry, 2018–2030

Agro-processing: Skills

Which level of skills is required due to 4IR adoption is likely to differ significantly by skill

Skills	Absolute change in percentage of workers requiring skill at level, 2018–2030 (%)		
	Basic	Intermediate	Advanced
Critical thinking and adaptive learning	–7.9	53.8	5.3
Written and verbal communication	–86.3	76.4	10.1
Numeracy	–46.0	–12.9	58.9
Complex problem solving	8.8	76.6	6.9
Management	–2.8	–12.8	15.6
Social	–91.1	77.2	14.0
Evaluation, judgment, and decision-making	–37.1	–32.1	69.2
Technical	–25.3	31.9	55.8
Computer literacy	74.4	–0.9	13.9
Digital/ICT skills	78.4	10.9	6.7

Legend: >50, >10, ≤10 ≥−10, < −10, < −50

4IR = Industry 4.0 or Fourth Industrial Revolution, GDP = gross domestic product, GSO = General Statistics Office (Viet Nam), ICT = information and communication technology, ILO = International Labour Organization, IMF = International Monetary Fund, LFS = Labour Force Surveys (Viet Nam), STEP = Systematic Tracking of Exchanges in Procurement.

Sources: Industry employment – GSO, LFS 2017 and ILO; GDP/Output – GSO, McKinsey and IMF Article IV; STEP survey data; Employer survey on impact of 4IR on the agro-processing industry in Viet Nam, n= 54+; Job portal data: jobs in the logistics industry scraped from the job portal VietnamWorks over the period from July to August 2019.

Box 6: Comparison of Insights in the Agro-Processing Industry Versus Past Research

Past research has examined the impact of Industry 4.0 (4IR) on the agro-processing industry in Viet Nam less than the logistics industry. The sector's limited ability to implement 4IR has been highlighted by the Ministry of Industry and Trade's assessment of 4IR readiness. This assessment scored agro-processing subsectors such as leather products manufacturing, food processing and textiles, significantly below other industries in terms of the number of firms that are of beginner or intermediate readiness for 4IR.[a]

While there is limited evidence on the employment impact in agro-processing, the findings in this research align with research conducted on the broader manufacturing industry in Viet Nam. Recent research by the Central Institute for Economic Management (CIEM) into the impact of 4IR for prioritized sectors estimated a 620,000 job-loss impact in the manufacturing sector under medium adoption of 4IR. This is consistent with the significant risk of job displacement modelled in this research.

[a] Ministry of Industry and Trade, UNDP. 2019. 4IR *Readiness of Industry Enterprises in Viet Nam*, https://www.vn.undp.org/content/Viet Nam/en/home/library/I40.html.

Source: CIEM internal document, unpublished. Findings were presented at a workshop in November 2018 in Ha Noi.

Skills Supply Trends

Figure 21 shows the breakdown of the additional demand for training that will be required by workers in the logistics industry under 4IR technology adoption. This reflects the volume of training required to bring the agro-processing workforce in Viet Nam from the skills required today in 2018, to the level of skills required by 2030, driven only by 4IR technology adoption. Longer formal training is estimated to play a much larger role in terms of training requirements for the agro-processing industry, as compared to the logistics industry. This is reflective of the large shift in skills development that is needed in the agro-processing industry, where on-the-job training may not suffice.

Though employers in both the agro-processing and logistics industries feel that there is a sufficient volume of graduates from relevant education and training programs to meet their company's entry-level hiring needs and over 50% of employers find it easy to identify high quality graduates (Figure 22), only 39% agreed (or strongly agreed) that graduates hired in the last year had been adequately prepared by their previous education or training.

Figure 21: Additional Person Trainings Required to Meet Skills Demand Driven by 4IR Adoption In Agro-Processing Industry in Viet Nam in 2030, by Type of Training

Agro-processing: Skills

Additional demand for training driven by 4IR adoption will likely need to be serviced with mostly on-the-job and longer formal training

Millions of person trainings required by type of training

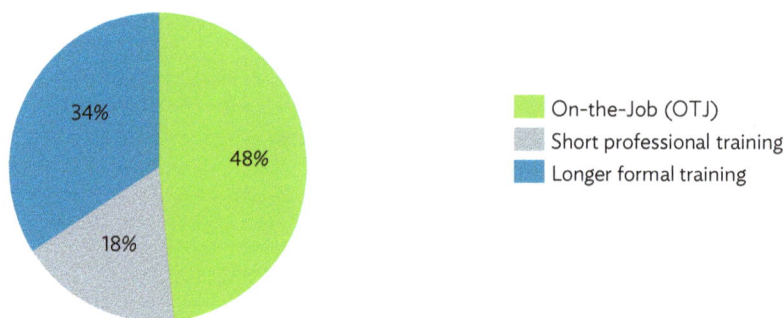

- 34%
- 48%
- 18%

- On-the-Job (OTJ)
- Short professional training
- Longer formal training

4IR = Industry 4.0 or Fourth Industrial Revolution, GDP = gross domestic product, GSO = General Statistics Office (Viet Nam), ILO = International Labour Organization, IMF = International Monetary Fund, LFS = Labour Force Surveys (Viet Nam), STEP = Systematic Tracking of Exchanges in Procurement.

Notes:

1. Figures include rounding adjustments.

2. One person training refers to training one worker, in one skill from the level required by his occupation's skill profile in 2018 to the relevant level given by the skills profile in 2030.

3. "On-the-job" training refers to training conducted during day to day such as senior staff instructing junior staff or running internal seminars; "Short professional" training refers to short (from 1 day to 6 months) courses conducted by professional internal or external instructors (e.g., weekend seminars, boot-camps). "Longer formal" trainings refer to trainings longer than 6 months for which workers would likely have to take leave from their jobs, these include returning into formal education such as obtaining a degree.

Source: Industry employment – GSO, LFS 2017 and ILO; GDP/Output – GSO, McKinsey and IMF Article IV; STEP survey data; Employer survey on impact of 4IR on the agro-processing industry in Viet Nam, n= 54+; Job portal data: jobs in the logistics industry scraped from the job portal VietnamWorks over the period from July to August 2019.

Figure 22: Employer Sentiment Toward Graduates Hired in the Past 24 Months

Agro-processing: Supply

While there seem to be enough graduates to fill positions in the industry, the education and training they have received may not be sufficient

Respondents (%)

Legend:
- Don't know (grey)
- Strongly disagree (dark orange)
- Disagree (orange)
- Neither agree nor disagree (dark grey)
- Agree (light blue)
- Strongly agree (green)

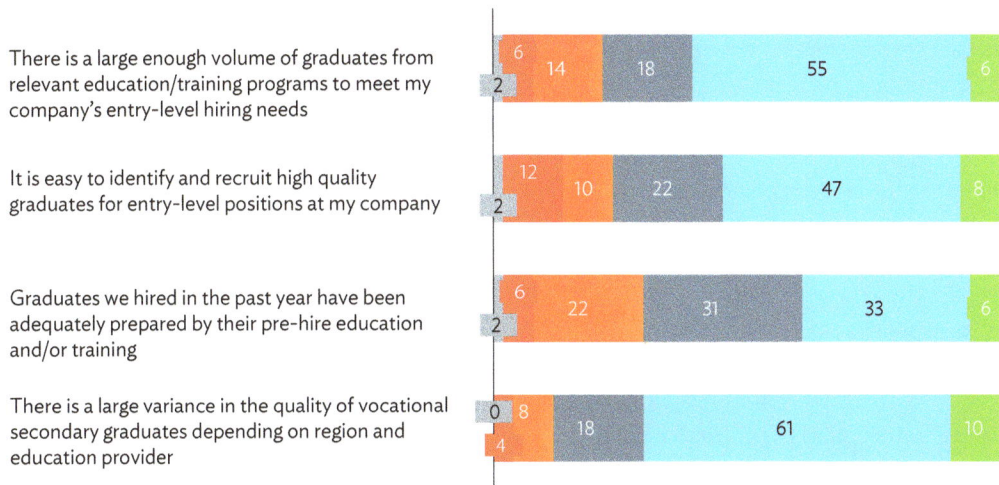

Statement	Strongly disagree	Disagree	Neither agree nor disagree	Agree	Strongly agree	Don't know
There is a large enough volume of graduates from relevant education/training programs to meet my company's entry-level hiring needs	6	14	18	55	6	2
It is easy to identify and recruit high quality graduates for entry-level positions at my company	12	10	22	47	8	2
Graduates we hired in the past year have been adequately prepared by their pre-hire education and/or training	6	22	31	33	6	2
There is a large variance in the quality of vocational secondary graduates depending on region and education provider	4	8	18	61	10	0

Source: Employer survey on impact of Industry 4.0 on the logistics industry in Viet Nam, n=51.

CHAPTER 2

Overview of the Training Landscape

This chapter provides insights into the performance of the TVET sector in Viet Nam as it deals with the challenges emerging from 4IR technology adoption. The insights are drawn from a survey of training institutions in Viet Nam, complemented with insights from the employer surveys discussed in Chapter 1.

There exists an evident mismatch between training institutions' expectations about graduates' preparedness for entry-level jobs and that of employers. While 80% of training institutions believe their graduates to be adequately prepared for the job market, less than 40% of employers agree. This gap exists despite training institutions' reportedly engaging frequently with industry. Training institutions in Viet Nam believe that policy actions around quality assurance mechanisms and further autonomy on the setting of standards and issuance of certification could support the sector in tackling 4IR.

To better understand the supply of talent and skills for the adoption of 4IR, a survey of training institutions was commissioned in Viet Nam, which included 74 institutions. The survey focused predominantly on TVET institutions of various levels of schooling. The majority of these are public institutions and, on average, 49% of their funding originates from public sources. Institutions of different sizes were sampled, with the smallest training fewer than 100 and the largest training ranging 20,000–50,000 students annually. The bulk of institutions trained about 1,000–10,000 students annually.

Industry 4.0 Readiness

Most institutions feel well prepared for 4IR; however, many are requesting additional technical and financial support (Figure 23). For example, close to 70% of institutions believe they have a good understanding of the skills needed to prepare graduates for 4IR technologies. Further, 66% of institutions claim to already have programs dedicated to 4IR skills, with 71% planning to develop or expand such programs by 2025. While 67% of institutions agree or strongly agree that they will be able to adequately prepare their graduates, 79% also agreed or strongly agreed that they needed additional technical and financial support, specifically for dealing with 4IR skills training.

Figure 23: Training Institutes' Perception of their Readiness for 4IR

Training sector: 4IR readiness

The majority of training institutions generally feel well-equipped for 4IR, however almost 80% will require some additional support

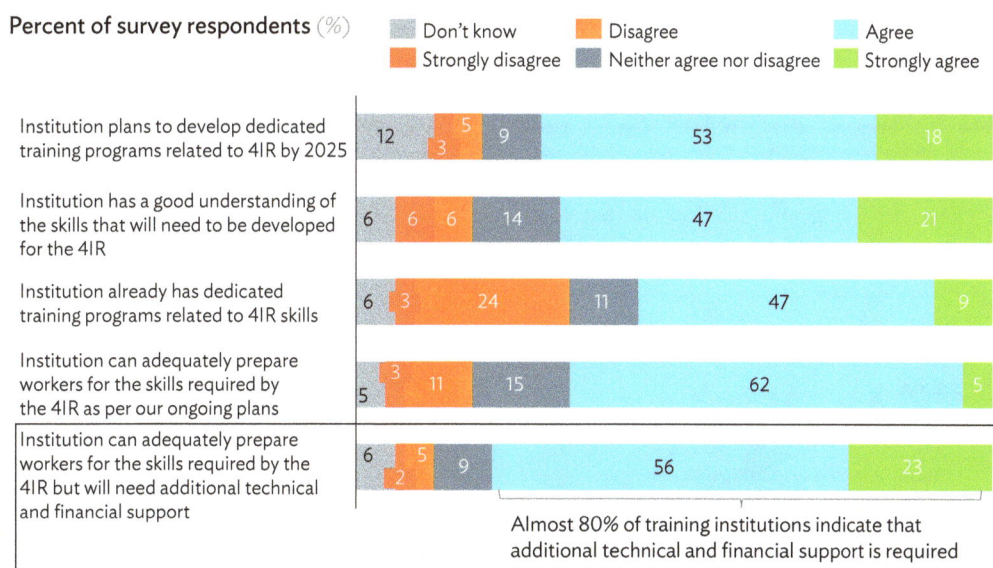

Percent of survey respondents (%)

Legend:
- Don't know
- Strongly disagree
- Disagree
- Neither agree nor disagree
- Agree
- Strongly agree

Statement	Don't know	Strongly disagree	Disagree	Neither agree nor disagree	Agree	Strongly agree
Institution plans to develop dedicated training programs related to 4IR by 2025	12	3	5	9	53	18
Institution has a good understanding of the skills that will need to be developed for the 4IR	6	6	6	14	47	21
Institution already has dedicated training programs related to 4IR skills	6	3	24	11	47	9
Institution can adequately prepare workers for the skills required by the 4IR as per our ongoing plans	5	3	11	15	62	5
Institution can adequately prepare workers for the skills required by the 4IR but will need additional technical and financial support	6	2	5	9	56	23

Almost 80% of training institutions indicate that additional technical and financial support is required

4IR = Industry 4.0 or Fourth Industrial Revolution.
Source: Training Institute survey on impact of 4IR in Viet Nam; n = 66.

More supporting evidence for the claim that institutions have a good understanding of 4IR requirements comes from the fact that their expectations of the importance of skills under 4IR aligns with those of employers, at least for the logistics and agro-processing industries (Figure 24). The skill category most training institutions believe will become much more important over the next 5 years is "evaluation, judgment and decision-making" skills, closely followed by digital/ICT, computer literacy skills, and management skills. This ranking resembles that provided by employers; however, employers emphasize far more than training institutions that digital/ICT, computer literacy, and technical skills will become important. On the other hand, fewer employers than training institutions believe that management skills will become more important in 5 years' time.

These results suggest that training institutes are broadly aware of the changes in skills required to support 4IR technology adoption, albeit with some differences in emphasis in certain skill categories between themselves and employers.

Figure 24: Potential Impact of 4IR on Importance of Different Skills Over the Next 5 Years

Training Sector: 4IR readiness

Training institutions and employers are generally aligned on which skills will become more important, however employers place greater focus on the importance on Digital/ICT, computer and technical skills

Percent of survey respondents (%)

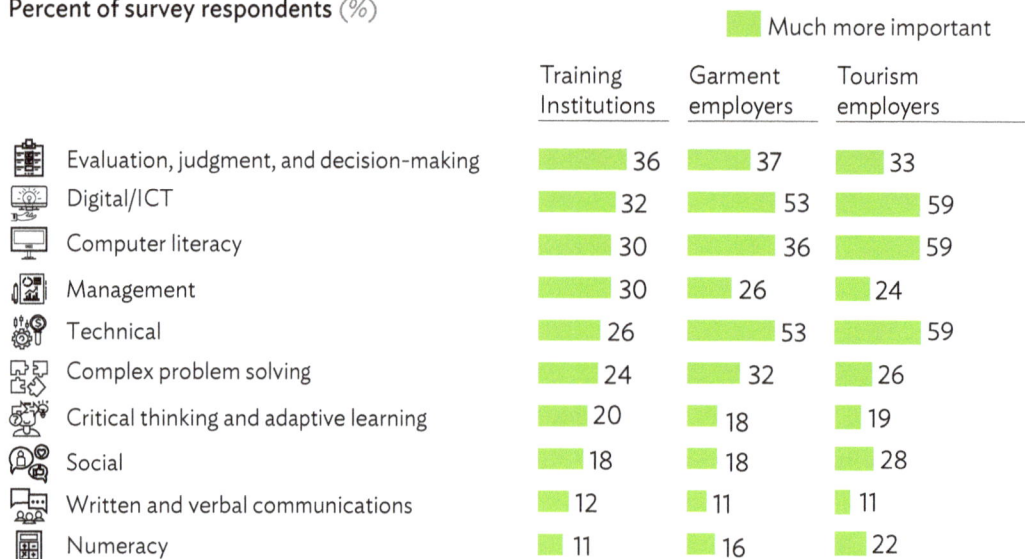

Much more important

	Training Institutions	Garment employers	Tourism employers
Evaluation, judgment, and decision-making	36	37	33
Digital/ICT	32	53	59
Computer literacy	30	36	59
Management	30	26	24
Technical	26	53	59
Complex problem solving	24	32	26
Critical thinking and adaptive learning	20	18	19
Social	18	18	28
Written and verbal communications	12	11	11
Numeracy	11	16	22

4IR = Industry 4.0 or Fourth Industrial Revolution, ICT = information and communication technology.

Source: Training Institute survey on impact of 4IR in Viet Nam; n = 66; Employer survey on impact of 4IR on the logistics industry in Viet Nam, n=57; Employer survey on impact of 4IR on the agro-processing industry in Viet Nam, n=54.

Curriculum

Aligning curricula with actual industry needs is one of the most important, but often most challenging, components of an effective training and education sector. It relies on frequent updating and close communication with industry, given the speed of change in 4IR technologies in the workplace. Regular curriculum reviews are therefore critical to keep pace with the skill changes related to 4IR. However, 47% of training institutions surveyed review and update their curricula less than annually (Figure 25).

Another concern is the content of the curriculum. During training, 46% of the time is spent on theoretical teaching and an additional 22% on classroom-based student projects with only a third of time being allocated to workplace-based training such as apprenticeships (Figure 26). This is in contrast to countries such as Denmark, Germany, Finland, France, Norway, and Switzerland who, at the upper secondary level, spend 50%–75% of instructional time on practical or on-site training.[31] This could pose a problem as survey evidence from Indonesia suggests that on-the-job training and hands-on learning are two of the top three most effective instructional techniques according to vocational students.[32]

---

[31]   M. Kuczera. 2010. *Learning for Jobs - The OECD International Survey of VET Systems: First Results and Technical Report.* https://www.oecd.org/education/skills-beyond-school/47334855.pdf.

[32]   Asia Philanthropy Circle. 2017. *Catalysing Productive Livelihood: A Guide to Education Interventions with an Accelerated Path to Scale and Impact.* https://www.edumap-indonesia.asiaphilanthropycircle.org/.

Figure 25: Frequency of Review and Update of Curricula by Training Institutions

Training Sector: Curriculum

Almost half of all training institutions review and update their curricula less than annually

Percent of survey respondents (%)

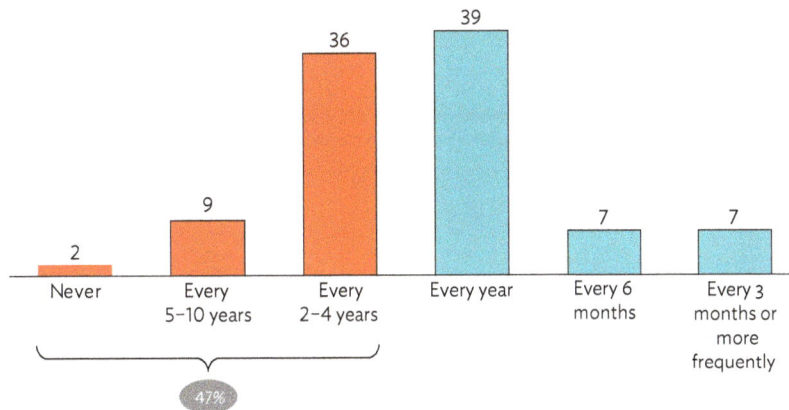

Source: Training Institute survey on impact of Industry 4.0 in Viet Nam; n = 56.

Figure 26: Share of Curriculum Time Spent by Type of Training

Training Sector: Curriculum

There is a lower focus on workplace or practical training than is seen in leading international vocational programs

Average percentage share of total time spent on training type at surveyed institutions (%)

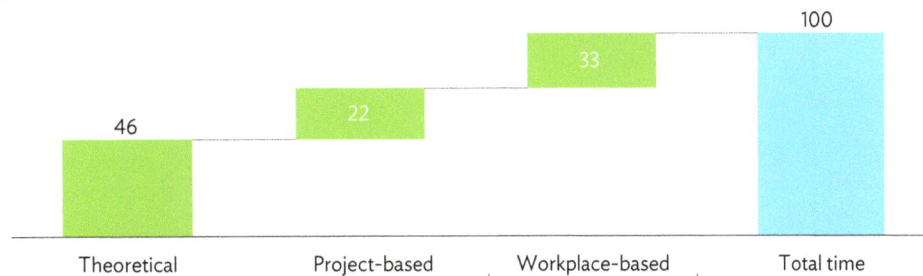

According to OECD research, more than three-quarters of vocational training programmes in Denmark, Germany, Finland, France, Norway, and Switzerland at the upper secondary level spend 50%–75% of instructional time in practical or on-site training.

OECD = Organisation for Economic Co-operation and Development.

Note: "Theoretical" training refers to lectures, "project based" refers to student projects, and "workplace-based" refers to on-the-job training such as industry apprenticeships.

Source: Training Institute survey on impact of Industry 4.0 in Viet Nam; n = 56; Małgorzata Kuczera, (2010), Learning for jobs - The OECD International Survey of VET Systems: First Results and Technical Report.

Interestingly, while the curriculum in most Vietnamese training institutions surveyed seems to provide courses relevant for 4IR, seemingly fewer institutions are adopting 4IR technologies themselves in the classroom (Figure 27). Of training institutions surveyed, 52% stated that they have rolled out courses specifically focusing on 4IR technology,[33] 46% have incorporated additional modules on 4IR-relevant skills into their conventional courses, and 39% are running digital programs at improving digital literacy. When it comes to technology adoption in the classroom however, current progress appears more limited. Only 45% of institutions make use of online self-learning tools; only 32% are employing some form of simulators for technical training; and only 4% of training institutes have adopted virtual learning platforms.

While the lack of technology use in the classroom is potentially linked to financial constraints, it appears that there is room for improvement in the frequency of curriculum revision and the use of technologies to more effectively deliver instruction linked to the curriculum.

Figure 27: Prevalence of Technology-Related Courses and Technology-Based Teaching Delivery at Training Institutions

Training Sector: Curriculum

Training institutions provide courses to teach 4IR relevant skills and technologies, but the uptake of 4IR in the classroom is largely limited

Prevalence of technology related courses at training institutions	Prevalence of technology-based delivery in teaching at training institutions
Percent of survey respondents (%)	Percent of survey respondents (%)

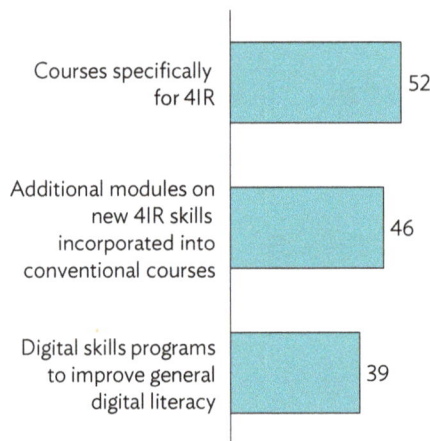

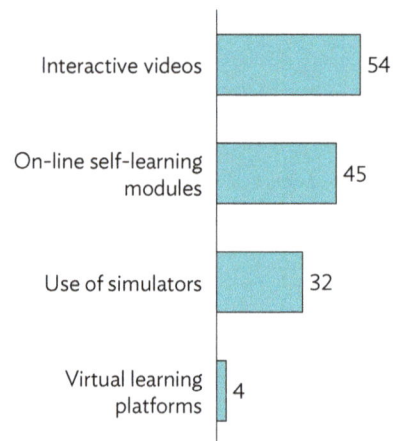

Courses specifically for 4IR	52
Additional modules on new 4IR skills incorporated into conventional courses	46
Digital skills programs to improve general digital literacy	39

Interactive videos	54
On-line self-learning modules	45
Use of simulators	32
Virtual learning platforms	4

4IR = Industry 4.0 or Fourth Industrial Revolution.
Source: Training Institute survey on impact of 4IR in Viet Nam; n = 56.

---

[33]   Note that, as opposed to the questions asked for Figure 11, this portion of the survey focused specifically on the hands-on use of technology in the classroom. Survey respondents were asked if their training institution already offers new courses specifically for 4IR technologies (e.g., educating on the use of 4IR technologies in specific industry sectors). Some institutions may have dedicated training programs related to 4IR skills, which could be soft skills (Figure 23), but have not gone as far as focusing on the use of 4IR technology/machines in courses, e.g., training students to work with or operate robotic manufacturing assistants, etc., or having such technology available for students. Hence, this more nuanced question was included in the survey.

Figure 28: Programs Provided in Addition to Training Courses

Training Sector: Curriculum

In addition to training courses, a number of training institutions provide programs such as career advice, scholarships, and company visits

Percent of survey respondents (%)

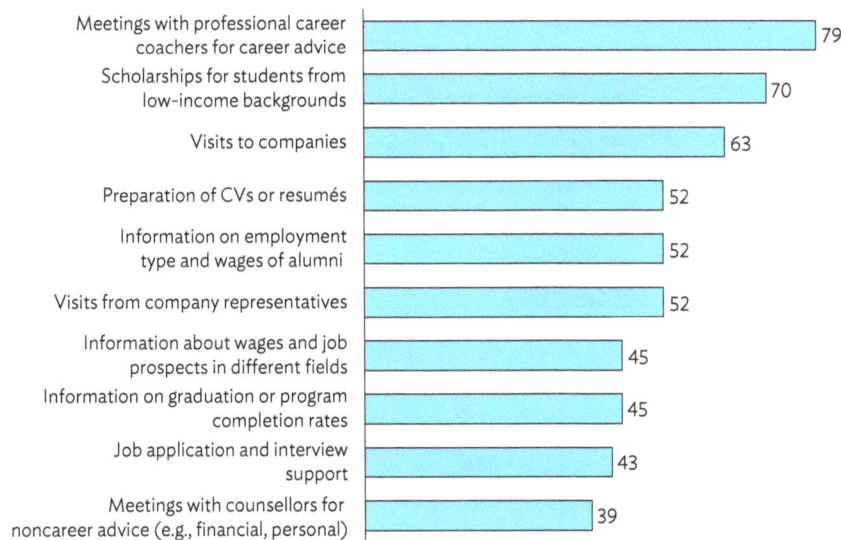

Meetings with professional career coaches for career advice	79
Scholarships for students from low-income backgrounds	70
Visits to companies	63
Preparation of CVs or resumés	52
Information on employment type and wages of alumni	52
Visits from company representatives	52
Information about wages and job prospects in different fields	45
Information on graduation or program completion rates	45
Job application and interview support	43
Meetings with counsellors for noncareer advice (e.g., financial, personal)	39

CV = curriculum vitae.
Source: Training institution survey on impact of Industry 4.0 in Viet Nam; n = 56.

Beyond the classroom, Vietnamese training institutions participate in several activities aimed at improving industry employment opportunities for their graduates (Figure 28). Of the surveyed institutions, 79% provide career guidance and 63% facilitate company visits and field trips for students. Where Vietnamese training institutions appear to struggle more is providing students with the right information to make informed career and life choices; only 52% inform students about the type of employment and wages earned by alumni, and 45% provide information on the type of employment and potential wages in different industries and occupations, as well as information on graduation rates. Only 39% provide noncareer advice and support for students such as financial and personal counselling.

Industry Engagement

Training institutions surveyed displayed very positive levels of interaction with potential employers, which contrasts with anecdotal evidence from targeted interviews with training institutions and from in-country consultation workshops. Of surveyed training institutions, 43% state that they communicate and coordinate with employers in relevant sectors several times a year and 36% state that they engage at least a couple of times a year (Figure 29).

Figure 29: Frequency of Communication with Employers in Relevant Sectors by Training Institutions

Training Sector: Employers

36% of training institutions communicate with employers less than 3 times a year

Percent of survey respondents (%)

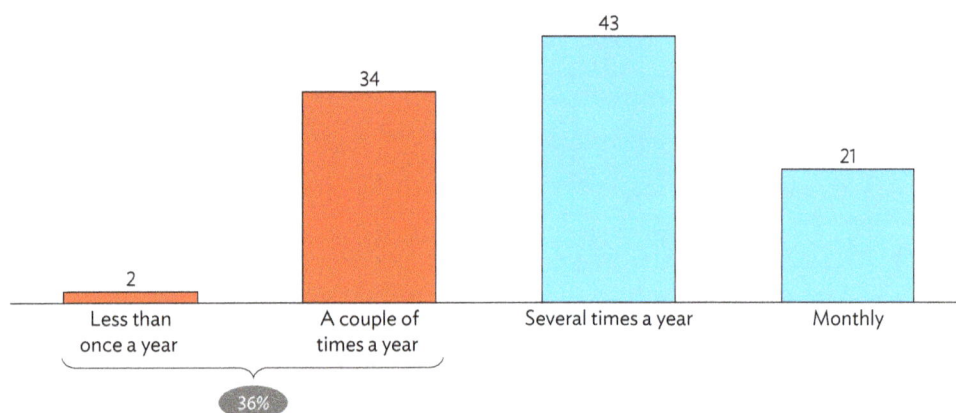

Note: May not add up to 100% due to rounding.

Source: Training Institute survey on impact of Industry 4.0 in the Viet Nam; n = 56.

Many training institutions (77%) indicated that they gathered input for curricula and worked with industry to organize internships for students (Figure 30). According to stakeholders at the country consultation workshop in Ha Noi in October 2019, TVET institutions in Viet Nam are increasingly placing a heavy focus on internships paired with "pay for performance" model where students do not pay if they do not match the skill requirements from firms (both tested during internships and after employment). This is particularly true for the food-processing industries. Unfortunately, not many make use of employer-provided equipment and facilities.

Employers in the surveyed sectors, logistics and agro-processing, are active in engaging training institutions (Figure 31). For example, 67% of surveyed firms in both industries offer internships, and 55% from the logistics industry and 61% from agro-processing participate in or organize job fairs. Even if employers are not currently engaged in activities, such as providing equipment and facilities, a large majority are willing to explore such models.

Figure 30: Potential Partnerships and Engagement Between Industry and Training Sector

Training Sector: Employers

Training institutions in Viet Nam report active engagement with employers with curriculum input and internships being most common

Percent of surveyed training institutions (%)

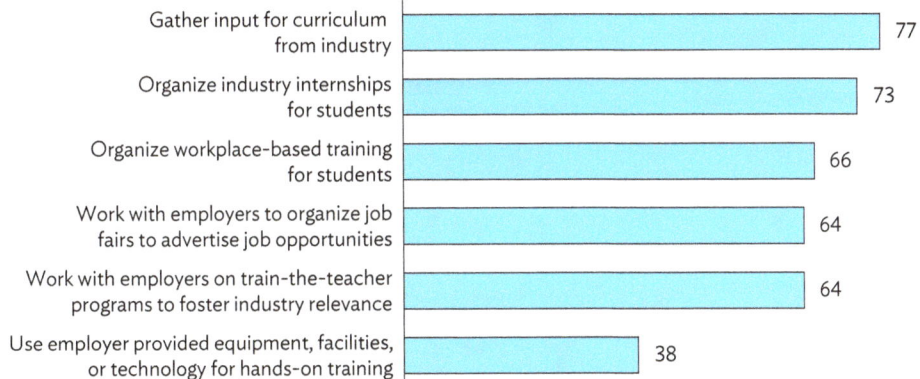

Gather input for curriculum from industry	77
Organize industry internships for students	73
Organize workplace-based training for students	66
Work with employers to organize job fairs to advertise job opportunities	64
Work with employers on train-the-teacher programs to foster industry relevance	64
Use employer provided equipment, facilities, or technology for hands-on training	38

Source: Training institution survey on impact of Industry 4.0 in Viet Nam; n = 56.

Figure 31: Potential Partnerships and Engagement Between Industry and Training Sector

Training Sector: Employers

Across the board, the industries appear active in engaging the training sector, and most employers are willing to explore new options

Percent of surveyed employers (%)   ■ Yes ■ No, but willing to explore this

	Logistics employers			Agro-processing employers		
	Yes	No, but willing	Total	Yes	No, but willing	Total
Offer student interships and apprenticeships	67	16	82	67	12	78
Participate in and/or organize job fairs to advertise job opportunities	55	20	75	61	12	73
Work with providers to determine what courses to offer	49	22	71	51	27	78
Provide input or otherwise helps to develop education and/or training curriculum	47	27	75	53	27	80
Provide train-the-teacher programs to teachers/instructors at training institutions	37	29	67	43	29	73
Provide equipment, facilities or technology for hands-on training to training institutions	35	33	69	41	29	71

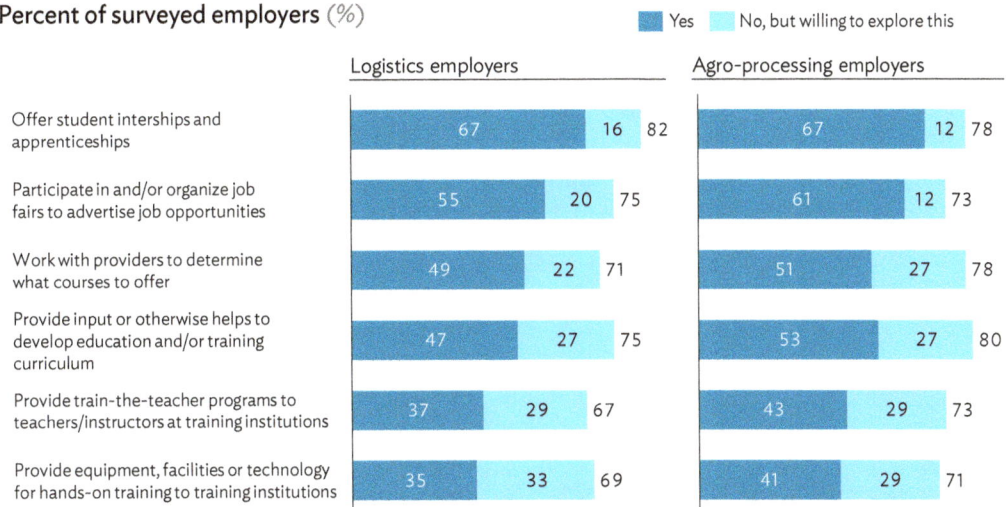

4IR = Industry 4.0 or Fourth Industrial Revolution.

Source: Employer survey on impact of 4IR on the logistics industry in Viet Nam, n = 51; Employer survey on impact of 4IR on the agroprocessing industry in Viet Nam, n = 51.

Figure 32: Current Annual Training Received While in Employment in Logistics and Agro-Processing in Viet Nam, by Trading Channel

Training Sector: Employers

Managerial, administrative, and customer-facing workers receive 1 day less of both formal and on-the-job training in the agro-processing industry

Training required by channel, days per year — Type of training | On-the-Job / Formal mid-career

Occupation	Logistics industry		Agro-processing industry	
	On-the-Job	Formal	On-the-Job	Formal
Managerial	8	8	7	7
Administrative	6	6	5	5
Technical	8	8	7	8
Manual job	7	6	6	6
Customer-facing	8	8	7	7

Source: Employer survey on impact of 4IR on the logistics industry in Viet Nam, n = 51; Employer survey on impact of 4IR on the agro-processing industry in Viet Nam, n = 51.

Employers in the surveyed sectors also appear reasonably active in employer-led training efforts. Of surveyed logistics businesses, 83% agree or strongly agree with the statement that most of their staff have received training in the past 12 months. While the number is lower for the agro-processing industry at 68%, this is still high. The amount of training received can differ by occupation and industry though. For example, workers in managerial, technical, and customer-facing roles in the logistics industry receive up to 8 days a year of professional and on-the-job training each (Figure 32). Administrative roles and manual jobs also receive at least 6 days of professional and on-the-job training each year. Employer-led training in the agro-processing industry appears lower across the board, in particular for administrative and customer-facing roles who on average receive 1 day less of professional and on-the-job training each.

Teachers, Trainers, and Instructors

It is encouraging to see that many training institutions are actively engaged in performance assessment of their teaching and training staff, with over 80% providing frequent feedback and formal annual/semi-annual performance reviews (Figure 33). Unfortunately, fewer institutions are developing their staff; 63% allow instructors to devote working hours to refresh their practical knowledge and/or learn new techniques on their own, and even fewer, 52%, provide ongoing professional development and industry-relevant training for instructors. Only 52% have regular visits from company representatives that could help with conveying new techniques to training staff.

Figure 33: Practices in Support of Institutions' Instructors and Teaching Staff

Training Sector: Instructors

On average, more training institutions are involved with instructor
and teacher assessment than with professional development

Percent of survey respondents (%)

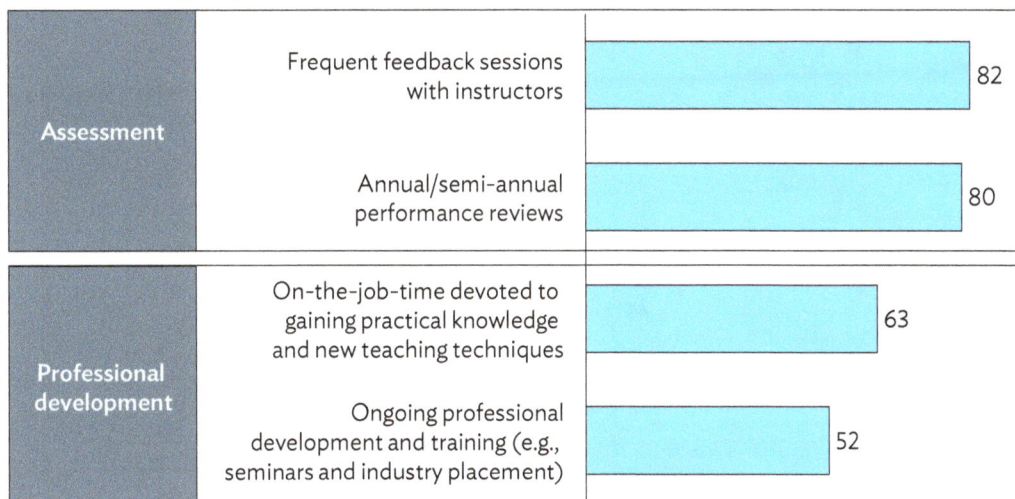

Assessment	Frequent feedback sessions with instructors	82
	Annual/semi-annual performance reviews	80
Professional development	On-the-job-time devoted to gaining practical knowledge and new teaching techniques	63
	Ongoing professional development and training (e.g., seminars and industry placement)	52

Source: Training Institute survey on impact of Industry 4.0 in Viet Nam; n = 56.

Performance and Policy Support

Of the training institutions surveyed, 72% face difficulties filling student spots and vacancies across their courses (Figure 34); 7% even experience extreme difficulties in doing so. The key reasons for these difficulties appear to be related to a lack of information among potential students. For example, 58% of the institutions facing difficulties in filling vacancies believe that an inability among trainees to differentiate programs and institutions by quality to be responsible for the low uptake. Further, 42% believe students do not perceive attending training institutions to be helpful to developing job-related skills and 39% see a lack of students' knowledge about the programs available to them as a key driver. This finding also emerged from a recent World Bank research in the logistics industry, which concluded that most potential candidates know little about the type of services offered by service providers, about career opportunities, and about the skills profile required by hiring firms.[34]

Training institutions' opinions on government policy are mostly positive (Figure 35). For example, 80% of training institutions feel that government policies on opening or expanding new programs have been beneficial for them. Further, 74% feel government funding of students is beneficial, while 18% even ascribe a strong positive effect.

---

[34] World Bank. 2019. *Viet Nam: Assessment of Logistics Skills, Training, and Competencies of Male and Female Employees.*

Figure 34: Difficulty to Fill Student Spots or Vacancies at Training Institutions

Training Sector: Policy

Over 70% of training institutions find it difficult to fill student vacancies, mostly as a result of a lack of information among potential trainees

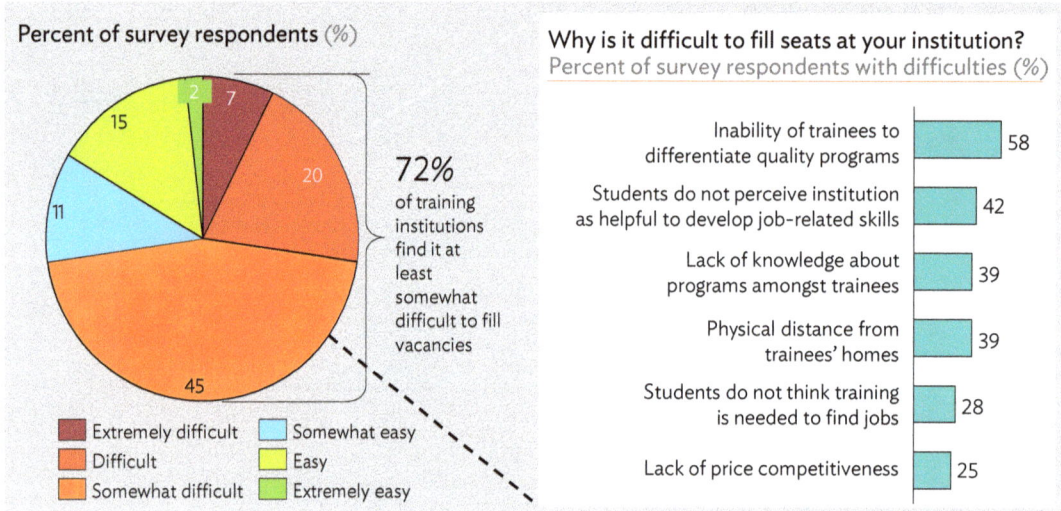

Percent of survey respondents (%)

72% of training institutions find it at least somewhat difficult to fill vacancies

- Extremely difficult
- Difficult
- Somewhat difficult
- Somewhat easy
- Easy
- Extremely easy

Why is it difficult to fill seats at your institution?
Percent of survey respondents with difficulties (%)

Inability of trainees to differentiate quality programs	58
Students do not perceive institution as helpful to develop job-related skills	42
Lack of knowledge about programs amongst trainees	39
Physical distance from trainees' homes	39
Students do not think training is needed to find jobs	28
Lack of price competitiveness	25

Source: Training Institute survey on impact of 4IR in Viet Nam; n = 53.

Figure 35: Training Institutions' Perception of Policy Effectiveness

Training Sector: Policy

Policy aimed at opening and expanding new programs as well as funding for students is deemed as most effective by training institutions

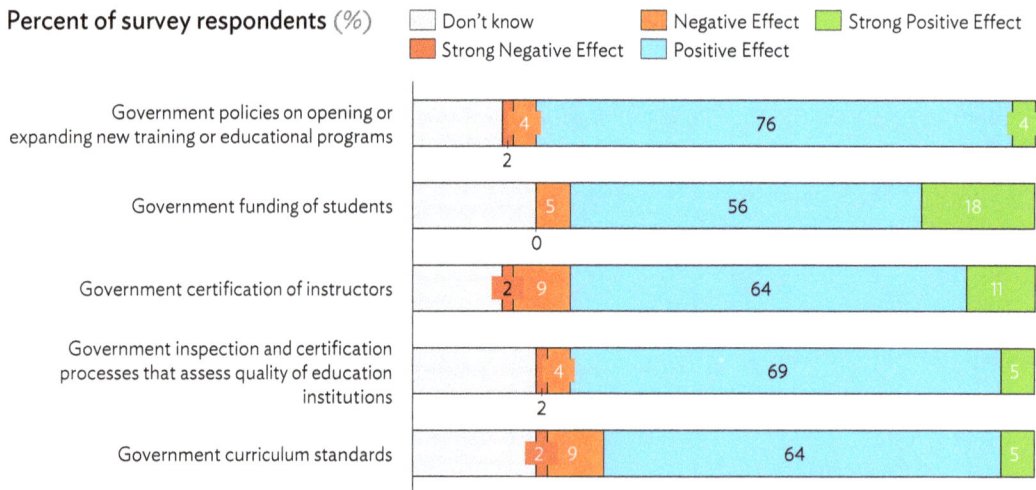

Percent of survey respondents (%)

- Don't know
- Strong Negative Effect
- Negative Effect
- Positive Effect
- Strong Positive Effect

Government policies on opening or expanding new training or educational programs: 2, 4, 76, 4
Government funding of students: 0, 5, 56, 18
Government certification of instructors: 2, 9, 64, 11
Government inspection and certification processes that assess quality of education institutions: 2, 4, 69, 5
Government curriculum standards: 2, 9, 64, 5

Source: Training institution survey on impact of Industry 4.0 in Viet Nam; n = 55.

Figure 36: Trainning Institute Perspective on Most Impactful Public Policies on Training Provision

Training Sector: Policy

Training institutions believe that quality assurance mechanisms and autonomy to set standards and certification would be most helpful policies

Percent of survey respondents (%)

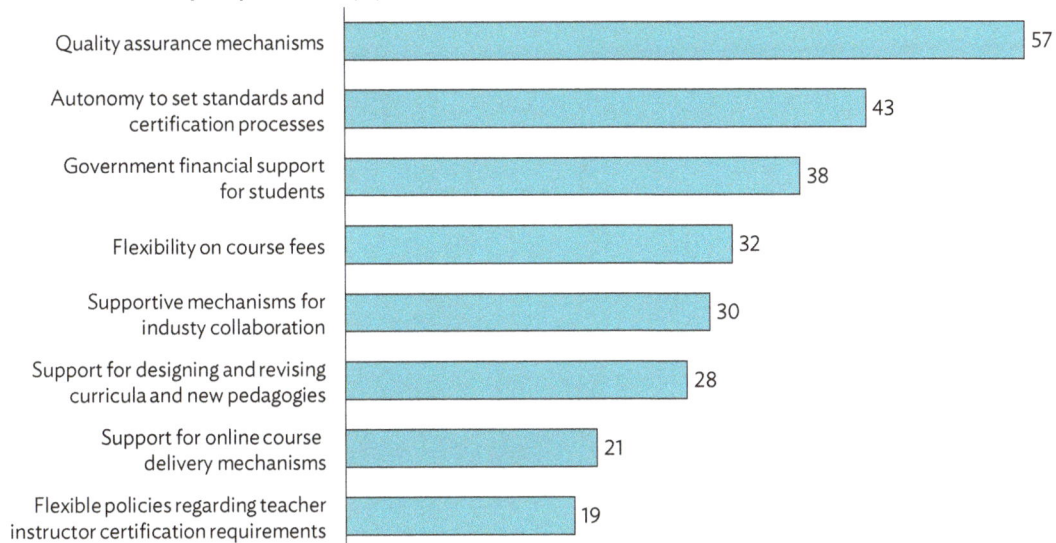

Policy	%
Quality assurance mechanisms	57
Autonomy to set standards and certification processes	43
Government financial support for students	38
Flexibility on course fees	32
Supportive mechanisms for industy collaboration	30
Support for designing and revising curricula and new pedagogies	28
Support for online course delivery mechanisms	21
Flexible policies regarding teacher instructor certification requirements	19

Source: Training Institute survey on impact of Industry 4.0 in Viet Nam; n = 53.

Training institutions are also looking to policymakers to address challenges (Figure 36). For example, 57% of institutions agree that government-enforced quality assurance mechanisms could (i) raise the quality of technical and vocational training, and (ii) give potential students the confidence in institutions' quality, combating above-described information failure. Further, autonomy for institutions to set their own standards and certification processes could align certification with industry requirements and address students' perception of training as not being helpful.

Supply and Demand Mismatches

As shown earlier, employers agree that there is a sufficient volume of graduates to meet entry-level hiring needs. Similarly, most training institutions (68%) agree there is enough demand from employers for graduates to ensure employment. As a result, training institutions reported that on average, 80% of their graduates find jobs after they graduate. However, there appear to be significant mismatches between the skills and certifications obtained by graduates, and those required by their prospective employers.

According to the training institutions surveyed, the most common reason why graduates may not be able to find a job is that the certifications provided are not well-recognized by employers (Figure 37). This finding could be linked to insights from the policy assessment, discussed in Chapter 3, that has found that there is a negative bias toward vocational education, favoring graduates with academic degrees,

Figure 37: Reasons for Students Being Unable to Find Employment Upon Graduation, by Prevalence

Training Sector: Students

Training institutions believe a lack of certification recognition and of preparation for jobs by training programs are key employment barriers

Ranking score, 1 - Most common; 5 - Least common

Rank		Average Ranking
1	Graduates' certifications are not well recognised by employers	2.2
2	Education and training programs do not adequately prepare job seekers for job opportunities	2.8
3	Not enough job opportunities	3.1
4	Enough jobs, but students unaware of job opportunities	3.4
5	Not enough opportunities for job seekers to complete relevant education or training for job opportunities	3.5

Source: Training Institute survey on impact of Industry 4.0 in the Viet Nam; n = 56.

which has led to an oversupply of degrees. The second most common reason is that graduates are not adequately prepared for the jobs they are looking for.

The second mismatch is with the actual skills, or the level of skills (i.e., basic, intermediate, advanced etc.) that graduates possess when they complete training or education. There seems to be a large misalignment between training institutions' expectation of graduate preparedness for work, and employers' expectations about graduates' skills required to perform well in entry-level roles. As Figure 38 shows, 80% of training institutes believe their graduates to be adequately prepared for entry-level positions. They also believe them to have the appropriate "general" skills and "job-specific" skills. This is in stark contrast to less than 40% of surveyed employers who agree or strongly agree with fresh graduates being adequately prepared for entry-level positions. While employers' perceptions of graduates' general and job-specific skills are better, they still fall short of training institutions' expectations.

This significant mismatch in skill expectations between employers and training institutions is particularly surprising given the high reported levels of engagement between employers and training institutions (noted earlier). These results suggest that while training institutions may have a good understanding of the skill categories of rising importance for 4IR (as shown in sub-chapter 2.1.1), the actual implementation of skill training, or depth and specific type of skills taught, do not match industry requirements.

Figure 38: Perception of Graduates' Preparedness for Entry-Level Positions

Training Sector: Students

On average, training institutions are more optimistic about the preparedness of graduates for work than what employers report

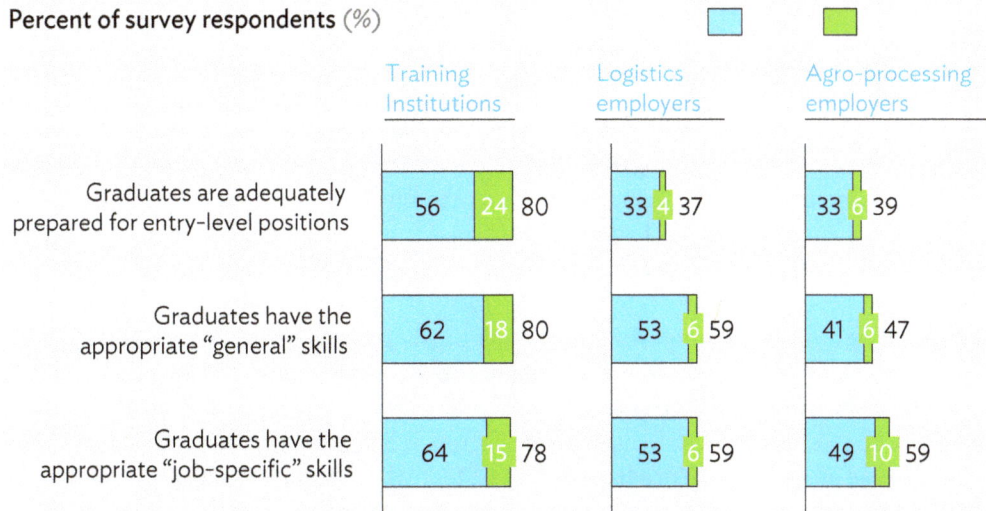

Percent of survey respondents (%)

	Training Institutions	Logistics employers	Agro-processing employers
Graduates are adequately prepared for entry-level positions	56 / 24 / 80	33 / 4 / 37	33 / 6 / 39
Graduates have the appropriate "general" skills	62 / 18 / 80	53 / 6 / 59	41 / 6 / 47
Graduates have the appropriate "job-specific" skills	64 / 15 / 78	53 / 6 / 59	49 / 10 / 59

4IR = Industry 4.0 or Fourth Industrial Revolution.

Source: Training Institute survey on impact of 4IR in Viet Nam, n = 55; Employer survey on impact of 4IR on the logistics industry in Viet Nam, n = 51; Employer survey on impact of 4IR on the agro-processing industry in Viet Nam, n = 51.

National Policy Responses

A thorough scan of all ongoing policies and programs by the government, industry, and civil society in Viet Nam reveals a range of strategies that seek to improve the readiness of the national workforce for 4IR. A considerable amount of focus has been placed on ensuring the relevance and agility of education and training curriculums to emerging skill needs, as well as in fostering closer collaboration between governments, industry, and civil society to create effective and relevant nationwide retraining frameworks. However, there appears to be weaker focus on several critical policy areas. These include ensuring a strong and even adoption of 4IR by firms, building awareness of "in demand" skills, creating incentives for employers and workers to participate in skills development, and inclusive models for underserved communities. While the success of the country's yet-to-be-published 4IR policy remains to be seen, significant effort appears to have been directed at ensuring this is forward-looking and robustly developed based on a local evidence base. However, there is scope for the improvement of coordination mechanisms between different government ministries and levels, as well as the alignment of government financing with strategic policy priorities.

The policy assessment leverages a combination of government documents relevant to 4IR and skills, academic literature, as well as relevant local surveys. These sources have been referenced throughout the report.

Overview of the Industry 4.0 Policy Landscape

Viet Nam has posted significant, steady growth over the last decades as the economy and population have benefited from a steady series of liberalizing economic reforms, starting with the Đổi Mới reforms of the 1980s. The leadership of the country understands that its own future is dependent on the continuation of this positive trajectory, and, overall, the policy direction trends in a progressive manner. Since the first articulation of the 4IR concept internationally, Viet Nam's leaders have embraced the notion, seeing adoption of its principles as the next logical evolution of the economy (and therefore the source of continued economic growth).

Thus far, this attention has manifested in the form of public statements from the Prime Minister and various others on the importance of 4IR; urging to various sectors, educational institutions, and government bodies to adopt 4IR; many forums and conferences on the topic; and even dedicated research and consulting projects. However, at this stage, such discussions remain in the abstract and lack concrete actions. A national strategy for 4IR is being drafted, but such documents in Viet Nam tend to be directional and provide general guidance; specifics on discrete policies and budget allocations will come only with more time.

That said, many parts of the government have been heading in the general direction of 4IR since before the concept was articulated as such. For instance, the opening of the country's vocational education system was already well underway and has made space for increases in collaboration with industry, more tailored curriculum, and a greater focus on skills. Relevant ministries have authored policies and directives that build on this momentum. Table 1 summarizes Viet Nam's key policy documents, with further information provided in the remainder of this chapter.

Table 1: Key Policies Relevant to Managing the Impact of 4IR on Skills in Viet Nam

Policy Document	Date	Responsible entity	Relevance
National Strategy for 4IR	TBD	Ministry of Planning and Investment/Central Institute for Economic Management	High-level direction on 4IR in most relevant areas
Resolution No.52-NQ/TW	2019	Politburo	"A number of guidelines and policies to actively participate in the Industrial Revolution 4.0" (quoted from Resolution)
Decision 999/QD-Ttg	2019	Ministry of Industry and Trade	Lays the groundwork for integrating flexible forms of labor more fully into the economy by instructing ministries to update and adapt regulations to the new technologies
Directive 16 "on the strengthening of the ability to access the Fourth Industrial Revolution"	2017	Ministry of Science and Technology; Ministry of Information and Communications	Assigned respective ministries to act in six specific areas to support 4IR
National Qualification Framework	2016	Ministry of Education and Training	Provides eight levels of qualifications mastery across sectors, designed to be compatible with the ASEAN Qualifications Reference Framework
Decision 761 on accrediting "High Quality TVET Institutions"	2014	Ministry of Labor, Invalids, and Social Affairs	The decision provided for aggressive investment in vocational school
Law on Vocational Education	2014	The National Assembly of Viet Nam	Governing law on vocational education
Decision 630 "approving the Vocational Training Development Strategy for the 2011-2020 period"	2012	Ministry of Labor, Invalids, and Social Affairs	Governing strategy for vocational training

4IR = Industry 4.0 or Fourth Industrial Revolution, ASEAN = Association of Southeast Asian Nations, TVET = technical vocational education and training.

Sources: Central Institute for Economic Management (CIEM) (2019), Draft National Strategy for 4IR (unpublished). Obtained from CIEM in August 2019; Vietnam Investment Review (2019), "Revolution to aid 4.0 breakthrough." https://www.vir.com.vn/resolution-to-aid-40-breakthrough-71065.html; Directorate of Vocational Education and Training (2019). http://gdnn.gov.vn/.

Viet Nam's government policies that are most relevant to the future of 4IR include:

(i)   **National Strategy to Promote Adoption of 4IR.** The country's strategy for 4IR is being drafted by the Central Institute for Economic Management (CIEM), a think tank belonging to the Ministry of Planning and Investment. The work is being informed by a number of research efforts and will examine impacts of nine technologies—including autonomous robots, IoT, augmented reality, and big data—and their relevance to the economy of Viet Nam using benchmarks from other countries. The current draft provides high-level direction in important areas like improving government response to 4IR, strengthening infrastructure and connectivity, improving higher and vocational education, and increasing research and development in relevant sectors.[35]

(ii) **Resolution No.52-NQ/TW (27 September 2019) of the Politburo on "A number of guidelines and policies to actively participate in the Industrial Revolution 4.0"** includes eight main guidelines. The fifth guideline is related to developing human resources, embedding minimum contents of digital and foreign language skills into education programs; innovating teaching and learning based on the application of digital technology; and continuing to improve mechanisms and policies to encourage, attract and develop high-quality human resources. The government will soon have an action plan for this Resolution.[36]

(iii) **Directive No. 16 on the Strengthening of the Ability to Access the Fourth Industrial Revolution (2017)** assigned respective ministries to act in six specific areas, including developing ICT infrastructure, supporting innovation, reforming science, technology, engineering, and math (STEM) and vocational education, and improving business conditions for companies.[37]

(iv) **Decision 761 on Accrediting "High Quality TVET Institutions" (2014)** provided for aggressive investment in vocational schools. The country selected 45 schools with a vision to meet specific criteria for "high quality" schools by 2020. This was done via investment in quality assurance, teacher and staff training, facilities, simulators, accreditation, certification, and digitalization, as well as granting greater financial autonomy (and preferential tax treatment) to the vocational school network. The program has yielded meaningful success.[38]

(v)   **Decision No. 630 on Approving the Vocational Training Development Strategy for the 2011–2020 Period**[39] is the current governing strategy for vocational training. It called for investments in the number of facilities and equipment, quality and quantity of programs or curriculum and teachers, promoting vocational professions, cooperation with businesses, and seeking international support. This has been updated and augmented in various ways, including a statement from the Directorate of Vocational Education and Training articulating strategies for supporting 4IR around improving training programs, developing teachers, and matching ASEAN standards for qualifications.[40]

---

[35] Central Institute for Economic Management (CIEM). 2019. *Draft National Strategy for 4IR* (unpublished). Obtained from CIEM in August 2019.

[36] *Vietnam Investment Review.* 2019. Revolution to Aid 4.0 Breakthrough. https://www.vir.com.vn/resolution-to-aid-40-breakthrough-71065.html.

[37] *Directive No. 16/CT-TTg on the strengthening of the ability to access the Fourth Industrial Revolution 2017.* https://vanbanphapluat.co/directive-16-ct-ttg-strengthening-of-the-ability-to-access-the-fourth-industrial-revolution.

[38] Based on stakeholder discussions in July 2019. *Trained in Viet Nam.* 2017. TVET Institutes Confirm Importance of Including Cooperation with the Business Sector in Criteria for High Quality TVET Institutes. 25 August. https://www.tvet-vietnam.org/en/article/1345.tvet-institutes-confirmimportance-of-including-cooperation-with-the-business-sector-in-criteria-for-high-quality-tvet-institutes.html.

[39] *Decision No. 630 / QD-TTg of the Prime Minister: Approving the Vocational Training Development Strategy for the 2011-2020 period.* http://gdnn.gov.vn/AIAdmin/News/View/tabid/66/newsid/5698/seo/Chien-luoc-phat-trien-Day-nghe-thoi-ky-2011--2020/Default.aspx.

[40] Directorate of Vocational Education and Training. 2018. *Manpower Training for Industrial Revolution 4.0.* http://gdnn.gov.vn/AIAdmin/News/View/tabid/66/newsid/36805/seo/Dao-tao-nhan-luc-cho-cach-mang-cong-nghiep-4-0/Default.aspx.

Assessment of Current Policy Approaches in Viet Nam Related to Industry 4.0

A diagnostic approach was taken to understand two important aspects of Viet Nam's 4IR policy approach: (i) "the what," that is, the specific policies being adopted by Viet Nam and how they compare to a set of international 4IR best practices; and (ii) "the how," that is, the implementation mechanisms.

Assessment of Policy Actions ("The What")

The country's policies and programs have been grouped into nine action areas assessed to be most crucial to managing the impact of Industry 4.0 on jobs and skills.[41] Figure 39 shows the current degree of focus by the country for each action area. The current degree of focus on each action area has been

Figure 39: Strength of Focus of Policy Actions to Manage the Impact of Industry 4.0 on Jobs and Skills in Viet Nam

Degree of current focus[a]: ■ Strong ■ Moderate □ Weak

Action agenda	Key action	Assessment
Stimulate Industry 4.0 adoption and worker	Ensure strong and even adoption of 4IR across firms and workers	Strong
	Build awareness of "in-demand" jobs and skills, as well as the benefits and opportunities of training	Moderate
	Incentivize employers and workers to participate in skills development	Moderate
	Foster close collaboration between governments, industry and civil society to create relevant and effective nationwide retraining frameworks	Moderate
Create new flexible qualification pathways	Establish effective lifelong learning models	Moderate
	Ensure relevance and agility of education and training curriculums to emerging skill needs	Moderate
	Encourage focus on skills rather than just qualifications in both recruitment and national labor market strategies	Moderate
Build inclusiveness to extend 4IR benefits to all workers	Build inclusive models that allow underserved groups to benefit from 4IR	Moderate
	Create social protection mechanisms for workers taking on flexible forms of labor	Moderate

4IR = Industry 4.0 or Fourth Industrial Revolution.

a   Degree of focus was assessed based on the following criteria: "Strong" – few or no gaps between the country's coverage of policy actions and coverage seen in international best practices; "Moderate" –medium level of gaps between the country's coverage of policy actions and coverage seen in international best practices; "Weak" – significant gaps between the country's coverage of policy actions and coverage seen in international best practices.

Source: Literature review; AlphaBeta analysis.

---

41   Based on AlphaBeta research on international best practices for policy actions that manage the impact of 4IR on jobs and skills. More details of these best practices can be found in Microsoft and AlphaBeta. 2019. *Preparing for AI: The Implications of Artificial Intelligence for Jobs and Skills in Asian Economies.* https://news.microsoft.com/apac/2019/08/26/preparing-for-ai-the-implications-of-artificial-intelligence-for-jobs-and-skills-in-asian-economies/.

rated as "strong", "moderate" or "weak" based on the analyzed extent of the policies' coverage in terms of scope and scale in comparison with those observed in international best practices.

Across the different actions of relevance for 4IR, Viet Nam has placed the strongest focus on ensuring the relevance and agility of education and the training curriculum to meet emerging skills needs. This can be seen in the many efforts already undertaken across primary, secondary, TVET, and tertiary programs to revise and strengthen the curriculum. Beyond this, there is good evidence that the country is strengthening lifelong learning models (e.g., the Viet Nam Association for Learning Promotion) and fostering collaboration between governments, industry, and civil society. Across the remaining actions, while Viet Nam has some activities in most areas, there are still significant opportunities to strengthen policy approaches. More specifically:

(i) **Stimulating industry adoption and worker reskilling.** Two key gaps in this area are the lack of awareness of in-demand jobs and skills; and the lack of strong incentives for firms to invest in training for 4IR. For example, 5% more employers in Viet Nam would rather hire new staff with the required skills than retrain existing workers; in addition, 68% of employers simply expect employees to pick up skills on the job.[42] There are similar gaps with knowledge of in-demand jobs and skills, and the required trainings. For example, 39% of training institutions (surveyed in Chapter 2) highlighted a lack of knowledge about programs among trainees as a key barrier to fill courses on 4IR.

(ii) **Creating new flexible qualification pathways.** In this area, Viet Nam has placed the strongest focus on ensuring training curricula meet emerging needs. Beyond this, there is good evidence that the country is strengthening lifelong learning models (e.g., the Viet Nam Association for Learning Promotion) and fostering collaboration between governments, industry, and civil society. However, many collaborations between industry and academia are still piecemeal and there is a lack of coordinated sector level efforts to align on key skills and qualification frameworks. Similarly, there is still a strong focus on traditional qualifications.

(iii) **Building inclusiveness to extend the benefits of 4IR to underserved communities.** Women and minorities are benefiting the least from the growing labor market, despite Viet Nam having one of the highest female workforce participation rates in the world (48%).[43] There are also large gaps in training rates of employees in urban areas (30.9%) versus rural areas (9.0%). In addition, given the currently limited social protection even for regular workers, there is still some way to go to protect on-demand, or flexible workers in the new economy.

Assessment of Implementation of Industry 4.0 Policies ("The How")
Implementation of Viet Nam 4IR strategy for jobs and skills was assessed against three dimensions found to be crucial for success according to past academic work: the clarity and robustness of plans, strength of coordination between different stakeholders, and the alignment of financing and incentives (Figure 40).[44]

42 World Economic Forum. 2018. The Future of Jobs Report 2018. http://www3.weforum.org/docs/WEF_Future_of_Jobs_2018.pdf.
43 Asian Development Bank. 2014. *Technical and Vocational Education and Training in the Socialist Republic of Viet Nam.* https://www. adb.org/publications/technical-and-vocational-education-and-training-socialist-republic-viet-nam-assessment.
44 Based on AlphaBeta research of Industry 4.0 strategies, plus insights from past public industry research, including: M. Barber. 2008. *Instruction to Deliver: Fighting to Transform Britain's Public Services;* E. Daly and S. Singham. 2012. Delivery 2.0: The New Challenge for Governments. *McKinsey & Company.* https://www.mckinsey.com/industries/public-sector/our-insights/delivery-20-the-new-challenge-for-governments.

Figure 40: Implementation Challenges Associated with Industry 4.0 Policies for Jobs and Skills in Viet Nam

Degree of current focus[a]: ■ Strong ■ Moderate ■ Weak

Dimension	Questions	Assessment
Clarity and robustness of plans	Is there a clearly articulated vision for 4IR?	Weak
	Is there strong integration between employment/skills and the 4IR plan?	Weak
	Is the plan forward looking, incorporating 4IR trends?	Strong
	Is there strong local data to support evidence-based policymaking?	Strong
Strength of coordination	Is there one shared roadmap across industry and government departments for Industry 4.0?	Moderate
	Is there coordination across different government ministries and levels?	Weak
	Is there strong alignment within and between industry, and education and training institutions?	Moderate
Alignment of financing and incentives	Is government financing aligned with the strategic goals?	Moderate
	What are the strength of incentives for employers and workers to invest in skill development? What are the strength of incentives for teachers and institutions to ensure high-quality training and education systems?	Weak

4IR = Industry 4.0 or Fourth Industrial Revolution.

[a] Degree of focus was assessed based on the following criteria: "Strong" –few or no gaps between the country's policy implementation approach and approach seen in international best practices; "Moderate" –medium level of gaps between the country's policy implementation approach and approach seen in international best practices; "Weak" –signifi cant gaps between the country's policy implementation approach and approach seen in international best practices.

Source: Literature review; AlphaBeta analysis.

The national strategies are still a work in progress and many of the elements above depend on that as a starting point. More specifically:

(i) **Clarity and robustness of plans.** Viet Nam's 4IR strategy is a work in progress. CIEM is currently finalizing a comprehensive national strategy for 4IR. A first draft has been completed, but it has not been made publicly available, so to date there is no formal direction or policy on 4IR.[45] Where there are directives, decisions, and policies relevant to future skills and/or 4IR, they tend to offer only high-level guidance without much specificity—e.g., urging leaders at all levels to improve awareness of job opportunities coming from vocational education.[46]

---

[45] Based on stakeholder discussion with CIEM, July 2019. (In 2018, Boston Consulting Group and CIEM laid the groundwork with an initial analysis on the economic and labor impacts of 4IR on Viet Nam.)

[46] For instance, *Decision No. 630 / QD-TTg of the Prime Minister: Approving the Vocational Training Development Strategy for the 2011-2020 period.* http://gdnn.gov.vn/AIAdmin/News/View/tabid/66/newsid/5698/seo/Chien-luoc-phat-trien-Day-nghe-thoi-ky-2011--2020/Default.aspx.

(ii) **Strength of coordination between different stakeholders.** For skills and education programs to be effective in responding to 4IR, it is critical that all stakeholders are coordinated and aligned on these programs, their objectives, implementation mechanisms and all related information. While the release of the National Strategy on 4IR in Viet Nam should help align all government stakeholders on a common approach, the level of coordination between different ministries and levels of government on implementing this policy and integrating it with other relevant policies will prove a meaningful test of the strategy's effectiveness. Alignment within and between industry and the training and education sectors on the skills demanded and the training required to supply them appears to be inadequate.

(iii) **Alignment of financing and incentives.** To date, there has been no direct financing or incentives for 4IR skills development beyond efforts to upgrade the educational system in general. Incentives for employers and current workers to engage more fully in upskilling are also limited.

CHAPTER 4

The Way Forward

The previous three chapters highlighted a series of challenges facing Viet Nam in relation to 4IR. This chapter summarizes those challenges and identifies several recommendations based on international best practices.

The COVID-19 Effect

The study was undertaken and completed prior to the spread of the coronavirus disease (COVID-19), which has caused unprecedented disruptions to global labor markets. This study's policy recommendations and strategies to strengthen widespread digital capabilities, enhance online or distant learning, digital platforms, education technology, and simulation-based learning have become all the more relevant in the aftermath of COVID-19. The key approaches discussed and elaborated in the report bear great relevance to the current context of countries experiencing nationwide closures of schools and training institutes. The expectation is also that, post-COVID-19, there would be operating procedures that constitute a "new normal" that entails far more digital capabilities in the workplace. Hence, the findings of this study and the follow-on policy directions are very timely and crucial for facilitating a sustainable COVID-19 strategy.

Viet Nam's agro-processing and logistics sectors have been extensively and adversely affected by COVID-19. In agro-processing, because of the pervasive impact on supply chains and value chains, the industry will need to rethink potential lasting shifts in consumer behavior in dealing with the COVID-19 response. Food retailers are likely to scale up e-commerce. The logistics part of the sector is likely to become more tech-oriented, calling for new skills and talent. The logistics sector itself is expected to experience a significant upswing due to COVID-19 arising from the growth of e-commerce and the changing nature of retail business due to the pandemic. A bounce-back strategy will entail embracing digital supply chains and launching digital sales and marketing initiatives. Hence the upskilling and reskilling on 4IR- related occupations is even more urgent for the revival of the economy and economic stimulus needed post-COVID-19.

The study obviously does not address the implications of COVID-19 in Viet Nam; however, the policy directions and future investments for higher order skills, particularly in the digital domain, are eminently suitable for the country to reimagine new beginnings for the two sectors.

Recap of Industry 4.0-Related Challenges Facing Viet Nam

Figure 41 recaps the challenges facing Viet Nam from the industry analysis (Chapter 1), the training institute survey (Chapter 2), and the policy assessment (Chapter 3).

Figure 41: Recap of Challenges Facing Viet Nam in Relation to 4IR

Area		Key challenges	Factoids
Sector-level analysis	1	Large displacement of workers in certain sectors, with large gender implications	26% and 33% of current workforce in logistics and agro-processing respectively could potentially be displaced by 4IR technologies
	2	Large shift in tasks and skill requirements	Agro-processing workers could be spending over 12% less time on routine physical tasks by 2030
	3	Significant ramp up of on-the-job training, particularly for analytical skills	48%–65% of new trainings related to 4IR will need to be delivered on-the-job
Training institute survey	4	Inability of trainees to differentiate quality of training programs	58% of training institutions highlighted this is the key reason for inability to fill courses on 4IR
	5	Mismatch on skill expectations	80% of training institutions believe graduates to be adequately prepared for job market, but less than 40% of employers agree
	6	Limited adoption of 4IR technologies in the classroom	Only 4% of training institutions are using virtual learning platforms
Policy assessment	7	Lack of flexible skill certification programs	Strong focus on traditional qualifications
	8	Lack of awareness of training opportunities	39% of training institutions highlighted a lack knowledge about programs among trainess as a key barrier to fill courses on 4IR
	9	Lack of incentives for inverstment by firms in working training	5% more employers would rather hire new staff with required skills than retain existing workers
	10	Lack of inclusive skilling oppotunities	There are also large gaps in training rated of employees in urban areas (–31%) versus rural areas (9%)

4IR = Industry 4.0 or Fourth Industrial Revolution.
Source: Asian Development Bank and AlphaBeta.

Recommendations to Address Challenges

Drawing upon international best practices, several recommendations have been outlined to strengthen Viet Nam's approach in terms of both policy scope and implementation processes (Figure 42). For each recommendation, a series of steps or possible approaches have been laid out as a practical roadmap for implementation in Viet Nam. Table 2 shows the key entity suggested to take the lead for each recommendation, as well as the other stakeholders to be involved. These entities span across the government, industry, education, and training sectors, reflecting the importance of strong multi-stakeholder partnerships for implementing them.

Recommendation 1: Develop Industry 4.0 transformation road maps for key sectors.
As the 4IR strategy is launched by Viet Nam, a practical starting point for its implementation could be to develop Singapore-style industry transformation maps (ITMs), which provide information on technology impacts, career pathways, the skills required for different occupations and reskilling options for different industries (Box 7). Industry-specific roadmaps for the logistics and agro-processing industries could be a useful starting point.

Table 2: Examples of 4IR Skills-Related Best Practices from Around the World

There are a range of relevant best practices that could be adopted to tackle these challenges

Recommendations	Common challenges	Examples of countries where recommendation was implemented
1 Develop 4IR transformation roadmaps for key sectors	• Large displacement of workers in certain sectors, with large gender implications • Large shift in tasks and skill requirements	– Australia, Singapore
2 Develop a series of industry-led TVET programs targeting skills for 4IR	• Mismatch on skills expectations • Significant ramp up of on-the-job training, particularly for analytical skills • Inability of trainees to differentiate quality of training programs	– Denmark, Finland, France, Germany, India, Norway, Switzerland
3 Upgrade training delivery through 4IR technology in classrooms and training facilities	• Limited adoption of 4IR technologies in the classroom	– Austria, Ireland, Switzerland
4 Develop flexible and modular skill certification programs	• Lack of flexible skill certification programs	– South Africa
5 Build programs to raise awareness of reskilling benefits, critical skills, and training opportunities	• Lack awareness of training opportunities	– Malaysia
6 Implement an incentive scheme for firms to train employees for 4IR	• Lack of incentives for investment by firms in worker training	– Malaysia, Singapore
7 Formulate new approaches and measures to strengthen inclusion and social protection in the context of 4IR	• Lack of inclusive skilling opportunities and social protection mechanisms for vulnerable workers	– Australia, Japan, Malaysia, Republic of Korea

4IR = Industry 4.0 or Fourth Industrial Revolution.

Source: Asian Development Bank and AlphaBeta.

This would include the creation of skills councils—employer-led organizations that would help support the development of occupational standards and qualifications frameworks in different industries. These skills councils could be led by a joint committee involving the Ministry of Industry and Trade (due to the link between 4IR and economic development), as well as the Ministry of Labor, Invalids and Social Affairs (due to the focus on workforce skills development). These councils would develop an understanding of the future skills needed in their industry, and contribute to occupational standards, apprenticeship frameworks, and qualification frameworks. During the country consultation workshop in Ha Noi in October 2019, the need to form effective skills councils was highlighted as a key area of reform. Interestingly, the employer and training institution surveys in this report highlighted that, despite significant reported engagements with industry by training institutions, there is a challenge with the recognition of qualifications by industry and the perceived quality of the graduates of training institutions. In December 2018, a Meeting of the Development Partners in Technical and Vocational Education and Training (TVET) Sector was held in Ha Noi to discuss skills councils and relevant international models.[47] In developing these roadmaps, there is a strong need for the ministries leading this effort to work closely with industry associations, employers with deep experience in training workers on 4IR skills, as well as training and higher education institutions in the country.

---

[47] TVET-Viet Nam. 2018. Industry Boards/ Skills Councils - A Mechanism Enhancing the Cooperation with the Business Sector in TVET. https://www.tvet-Viet Nam.org/en/article/1569.industry-boards-skills-councils-a-mechanism-enhancing-the-cooperation-with-the-business-sector-in-tvet.html.

Table 3: Suggested Leads and Stakeholders to Engage for Potential Actions in the Recommendations to Strengthen the 4IR Approach

No.	Recommendation	Key Suggested Lead/s	Stakeholders to Involve
1	Develop 4IR transformation roadmaps for key sectors	Joint committee constituting the Ministry of Industry and Trade and the Ministry of Labor, Invalids and Social Affairs	• Industry associations (including representatives from key employers in each sector) • Training institutions • Higher education institutions
2	Develop a series of industry-led TVET programs targeting skills for 4IR	Key employers in each industry	• Training institutions • Educational institutions • Ministry of Labor, Invalids and Social Affairs
3	Upgrade training delivery through 4IR technology in classrooms and training facilities	Ministry of Education and Training	• Ministry of Science and Technology • Education technology ("EdTech") companies
4	Develop flexible and modular skill certification programs	Ministry of Labor, Invalids and Social Affairs and Ministry of Education and Training	• Industry associations (including representatives from key companies with strong training programs in each sector) • Training institutions
5	Build programs to raise awareness of reskilling benefits, critical skills, and training opportunities	Ministry of Labor, Invalids and Social Affairs	• Ministry of Education and Training • Industry and employer associations
6	Implement an incentive scheme for firms to train employees for 4IR	Joint committee including the Ministry of Planning and Investment, Ministry of Industry and Trade, Ministry of Labor, Invalids and Social Affairs, and Ministry of Education and Training	• Industry associations (including key employers in each industry)
7	Formulate new approaches and measures to strengthen inclusion and social protection in the context of 4IR	Ministry of Labor, Invalids and Social Affairs	• Ministry of Education and Training • Ministry of Trade and Industry • Industry associations (including key employers in each industry) • Nonprofit organizations

4IR = Industry 4.0 or Fourth Industrial Revolution, TVET = technical and vocational education and training.
Source: Asian Development Bank and AlphaBeta.

> ### Box 7: Singapore's Industry Transformation Maps
>
> Singapore's Industry 4.0 (4IR) effort, comprising the industry transformation maps (ITMs), is overseen by a dedicated body: the Future Economy Council. Chaired by the Deputy Prime Minister, the Future Economy Council is represented by members from the government, industry, unions and educational and training institutes. Each ITM represents the roadmap to 4IR technology adoption for an industry sector. To ensure coordination and accountability within the government, each ITM is championed by a different government agency whose purview is most relevant to the sector. For example, the ITM for the manufacturing sector is led by the Economic Development Agency, while that for the built environment sector is led by the Building and Construction Authority.
>
> The "Skills Framework" is a key component of the ITMs. Co-created by industry, government, and civil society actors, the framework provides key information on career pathways, the existing and emerging skills required for different occupations and reskilling options for different sectors. It also provides a list of training programs for skills upgrading. By virtue of its multi-stakeholder nature, this framework is also intended to benefit not just workers, but also employers. A 2018 survey of over 700 firms in Singapore found that 36% take guidance from the ITMs on how to improve their talent pipeline, and how they could address manpower challenges for different sectors.
>
> [a] Government of Singapore, Ministry of Trade and Industry. 2020. The Future Economy Council. https://www.mti.gov.sg/FutureEconomy/TheFutureEconomyCouncil; and Government of Singapore, Ministry of Education. 2016. Press release: Formation of the Council for Skills, Innovation and Productivity. https://www.moe.gov.sg/news/press-releases/formation-of-the-council-for-skills--innovation-and-productivity.
>
> [b] Government of Singapore, Ministry of Trade and Industry. 2017. *Media Factsheet- Industry Transformation Maps.* https://www.mti.gov.sg/-/media/MTI/ITM/General/Fact-sheet-on-Industry-Transformation-Maps---revised-as-of-31-Mar-17.pdf.
>
> [c] Government of Singapore, Ministry of Trade and Industry. 2017. *Media Factsheet- Industry Transformation Maps.* https://www.mti.gov.sg/-/media/MTI/ITM/General/Fact-sheet-on-Industry-Transformation-Maps---revised-as-of-31-Mar-17.pdf.
>
> [d] S. K. Tang. 2019. Singapore Businesses Not Investing Enough in Employee Training: SBF Survey. *Channel News Asia.* https://www.channelnewsasia.com/news/business/singapore-companies-not-investing-employee-training-sbf-survey-11134230.
>
> Source: Asian Development Bank and AlphaBeta.

Recommendation 2: Develop a series of industry-led TVET programs targeting skills for Industry 4.0.

The poor quality of TVET programs and their lack of industry relevance was identified in the employer surveys (Chapter 1) and in the training institute survey (Chapter 2). A review of Viet Nam's quality assurance systems for TVET also highlighted the lack of industry involvement.[48] Strengthening the quality and relevance of TVET programs vis-à-vis the agro-processing and logistics industries is in line with the suggested actions from a report by the Vietnam Logistics Business Association (VLA) and the Vietnam Logistics Research and Development Institute (VLI), which called for training institutions to sign strategic contracts with logistics enterprises to develop human resources that meet specific skill needs related to 4IR.[49]

---

[48] United Nations Educational, Scientific and Cultural Organization (UNESCO). 2017. *Towards Quality Assurance of Technical and Vocational Education and Training.* https://unesdoc.unesco.org/ark:/48223/pf0000259282.

[49] AusAid, VLA, VLI. 2019. *Brief Report on the Current Status of the Logistics Workforce in Viet Nam.*

Box 8: Connecting Students and Industry with Boot Camps

Industry needs appropriately trained recruits, and youth job seekers need to be hired. Boot camps can connect the skills offered by young job seekers to those needed by industry. The "Generation Program" focuses on four industries with teaching facilities in 119 cities in six continents. The program is offered to 18- to 29-year-olds. Among the program's features are direct contact with potential employers, matching trainee attributes with employer needs, courses that cover technical, behavioral, and mental skills, continuous monitoring, and support during and after the program, and a strong alumni network.

Since its inception, 31,600 people have gone through the training with 80% finding jobs within 3 months of finishing the program and 65% of those stayed with their jobs for at least 1 year.[a] Employers also rate program graduates as higher performing than their peers.

[a] Generation Program. 2019. https://www.generation.org/.

Source: Asian Development Bank and AlphaBeta.

Industry-led TVET programs could work together with industry associations and education institutions to scope them, with support by the Ministry of Labor, Invalids and Social Affairs. Parameters, potentially informed by international best practices, could include training curricula and their durations, teacher recruitment and training, and applicant criteria. Some notable examples include industry bootcamps by McKinsey & Company's Generation program, which operates across several countries (Box 8) (footnote 32).

Recommendation 3: Upgrade training delivery through Industry 4.0 technology in classrooms and training facilities.

The survey of training institutions in Chapter 2 revealed that, while many training institutions are using some technologies such as online learning modules, few are using other technologies such as virtual or augmented reality. There are a range of new technologies that could support 4IR instruction in Viet Nam. Artifical Intelligence (AI) technology, for example, has been used to stimulate critical thinking through applying a virtual environment for building and assessing higher order inquiry skills.[50] AI-enabled immersive computer games have also been used for science, technology, engineering, and mathematics (STEM) education in some schools in the United States.[51]

This is an area in which the Ministry of Education and Training can take the lead with the Ministry of Science and Technology, as well as education technology firms in the country, to incorporate 4IR technologies in classrooms from elementary schools to universities and polytechnics. As installing such technologies and equipment at every institution could be fiscally challenging, a possible way to manage costs while maximizing their benefits is to adopt blended learning approaches. Such approaches combine both classroom and personalized online learning and have been demonstrated to be highly effective at not just improving education outcomes but also addressing gender inequality (Box 9).

---

[50] J. M. Spector and S. Ma. 2019. Inquiry and Critical Thinking Skills for the Next Generation: From Artificial Intelligence Back to Human Intelligence. *Smart Learning Environments*. https://slejournal.springeropen.com/articles/10.1186/s40561-019-0088-z.

[51] D. J. Ketelhut et al. 2009. A Multi-User Virtual Environment for Building and Assessing Higher Order Inquiry Skills in Science. *British Journal of Educational Technology*. https://onlinelibrary.wiley.com/doi/abs/10.1111/j.1467-8535.2009.01036.x.

Box 9: Leveraging Technologies to Improve Education and Address Gender Inequality

Digital technologies have been shown to improve education quality and even manage gender gaps starting from at an early age.

The African School for Excellence (ASE), an affordable private secondary school in South Africa, deploys an innovative rotational classroom model in which students rotate between teacher-facilitated lessons, small-group peer-learning activities, and individual work on computers supervised by trainee teachers. Deploying online courses from free products such as the Khan Academy, this blended learning approach innovatively reduces costs through its reliance on a smaller number of highly trained teachers, while enhancing education outcomes with its emphasis on personalized learning and small class sizes. ASE students have been found to outperform the wealthiest students in the country by 2.3 times in mathematics and 1.4 times in English.[a]
At the same time, the per-student cost of US$800 a year is low when compared with South African averages of $1,400–$16,500 per year (footnote a).

Such personalized adaptive learning digital tools are also beginning to show their potential in bridging gender differences in students' attainment from a young age. "onebillion," a London-based nonprofit organization focused on building scalable educational software for children, launched the app "onecourse," which delivers content and practice on a tablet.[b] This app was found to prevent a gender gap in reading and mathematics skills among first-grade students in Malawi, potentially by overcoming sociocultural factors responsible for gaps emerging in traditional classroom settings.[c]

[a] Center for Universal Education at Brookings. 2019. *Learning to Leapfrog: Innovative Pedagogies to Transform Education.* https://www.brookings.edu/wp-content/uploads/2019/09/Learning-to-Leapfrog-InnovativePedagogiestoTransformEducation-Web.pdf.

[b] onebillion. Onecourse: One App That Delivers Reading, Writing And Numeracy. https://onebillion.org/onecourse/app/.

[c] Pathways for Prosperity Commission. 2019. *Positive Disruption: Health and Education in the Digital Age.* https://pathwayscommission.bsg.ox.ac.uk/positive-disruption.

Source: Asian Development Bank and AlphaBeta.

Recommendation 4: Develop flexible and modular skill certification programs.

As outlined in Chapter 3, there is still a strong emphasis on traditional qualifications attained through the education system or competency assessments. This recommendation thus encourages a stronger focus on skills—beyond such traditional qualifications—including in both the agro-processing and logistics industries. The Ministry of Labor, Invalids, and Social Affairs could lead this initiative jointly with the Ministry of Education and Training. This initiative would involve (i) reviewing the need for minimum educational qualifications and competency-based assessments in current certification frameworks (together with industry and training institutions); (ii) analyzing the potential impact of complementing or partially replacing such criteria with evidence of skills attainment from pathways such as accredited training programs, industry apprenticeships, and certificates recognizing learning through past work experience (potentially taking reference from Malaysia's Skills Certification Framework, Box 10); and (iii) synchronizing these processes with the conventional certifications based on academic qualifications (ensuring they are recognized by employers).

Box 10: The Malaysian Skills Certification Program

In Malaysia, individuals who do not possess formal educational qualifications can enter into their desired careers through the Malaysian Skills Certification Program.

Recognized by industry, this program awards skills certificates at five different levels:

(i)   Malaysian Skills Certificate Level 1
(ii)   Malaysian Skills Certificate Level 2
(iii)   Malaysian Skills Certificate Level 3
(iv)   Diploma in Skills Malaysia Level 4
(v)   Malaysian Skills Advanced Diploma Level 5[a]

These certificates are awarded across all industries of the economy, classified into 22 industries, according to the country's "National Occupational Skills Standard."[b] Importantly, no former educational qualifications are required—the only requirements for candidates are the ability to speak and write in both Bahasa Melayu and English, and the need to have passed a lower Skills Certificate level before being able to qualify for a higher level in the same field.

Candidates may obtain these certificates through three channels: training in institutions accredited by the *Jabatan Pembangunan Kemahiran* (Department of Skills Development); industry apprenticeships under the National Dual Training System; and through sufficient "Accreditation of Prior Achievement" (footnote a). The third channel refers to accreditation gained through evidence of past work and/or training experience.

With these certificates being accredited as officially recognized qualifications and mapped to equivalent academic qualifications under the Malaysian Qualifications Framework, Malaysian companies are able to take guidance from this framework when assessing the suitability of job candidates without formal education but who possess the relevant skills to excel at the job.[c]

[a] Department of Skills Department. *Malaysian Skill Certificate (SKM)*. https://www.dsd.gov.my/jpkv4/index.php/en/malaysian-skills-certificate.

[b] Organisation for Economic Co-operation and Development. 2012. *Skills Development Pathways in Asia*. https://www.oecd.org/cfe/leed/Skills%20Development%20Pathways%20in%20Asia_FINAL%20VERSION.pdf

[c] Ministry of Higher Education and Malaysian Qualifications Agency. 2011. *Malaysian Qualifications Framework*. http://www2.mqa.gov.my/mobile/mqf.html.

Source: Asian Development Bank and AlphaBeta.

Recommendation 5: Build programs to raise awareness of reskilling benefits, critical skills, and training opportunities.

Viet Nam possesses a young, highly motivated, and hard-working labor force, but there is a general lack of awareness among workers of in-demand and future skills; lack of awareness was highlighted as one of the key challenges in Chapter 2. The country would benefit from a comprehensive approach to increasing awareness of reskilling benefits for employees and employers alike.

Box 11: International Approaches to Sharing Information on In-Demand Skills

Online technology is being used to provide easily accessible, up-to-date information on in-demand skills. Examples include:

(i)   The Government of New Zealand developed a mobile app called "Occupation Outlook," which allows residents to explore study and career options based on extensive information on labor supply and demand in over 100 occupations in New Zealand. By outlining the qualifications required for each role, average incomes, as well as job prospects upon completion of the required qualifications, it allows New Zealanders to make informed decisions about their education and career.[a]

(ii)   LinkedIn partnered with the World Bank to establish an interactive online skill–to–industry mapping database, which was launched in April 2019.[b] This is a comprehensive, free online tool that leverages LinkedIn data covering over 100 countries with at least 100,000 LinkedIn members each, and distributed across 148 industries and 50,000 skills categories. This tool allows both policymakers and workers to understand global shifts in skill requirements by industry, the portability of skills across sectors, as well as country-level trends in sectoral employment and talent migration.[c]

[a] Ministry of Business, Innovation and Employment, New Zealand. 2019. Occupation Outlook. http://occupationoutlook.mbie.govt.nz/

[b] World Bank Group and LinkedIn Corporation, World Bank LinkedIn Digital Data for Development, licensed under CC BY 3.0. https://linkedindata.worldbank.org/ (accessed 7 July 2020).

[c] World Bank Group and LinkedIn Corporation. *Data Insights: Jobs, Skills and Migration Trends Methodology and Validation Results.* https://datacatalog.worldbank.org/dataset/world-bank-group-linkedin-dashboard-dataset#tab2 (accessed 7 July 2020).

Source: Asian Development Bank and AlphaBeta.

Elements of such a program could include:

(i)   **Develop real-time online information and mobile applications on in-demand skills.**
Viet Nam could develop up-to-date online information about the current labor market, including salaries, skill requirements, and demand trends. Box 11 provides some examples that could inform the design of this effort. A starting point would be to conduct a survey to understand how students and workers currently find labor market information and the challenges they encounter, and to conduct a detailed landscape review of any sources of information. This could then inform the design of this online depository.

(ii)   **Develop an outreach program to inform workers and employers of available skills training and support.** The Government of Singapore has established a dedicated unit to educate firms about worker reskilling needs and opportunities under the government's skills training courses.[52] A starting point in Viet Nam could be to develop an approach for one particular sector (e.g., logistics or agro-processing), which would include sharing information on skill demand trends, available courses, and training support. A randomized control trial could measure changes in uptake of training in these sectors versus other sectors. Subject to the results, this approach could then be refined and scaled to other sectors, incorporating the relevant lessons from this pilot.

---

[52]   F. Mokhtar. 2018. SkillsFuture Singapore to Deepen Skills of Training and Adult Education Providers. *Today.* https://www.todayonline.com/singapore/skillsfuture-singapore-deepen-skills-training-and-adult-education-providers.

This initiative could be led by the Ministry of Labor, Invalids and Social Affairs, and given the strong implications for education policy and curricula it is recommended that this is done in close consultation with the Ministry of Education and Training. To ensure that a thorough understanding of skill needs is forged in this framework, industry and employer associations should be consulted or brought in as part of a public–private taskforce.

Recommendation 6: Implement an incentive scheme for firms to train employees for Industry 4.0.

Despite the substantial productivity gains 4IR technologies could bring about (as demonstrated in Chapter 1), employer-led training efforts in Viet Nam remain limited. A recent survey showed that 5% more employers in Viet Nam would rather hire new staff with the required skills than retrain existing workers, and that 68% of employers simply expect employees to pick up skills on the job.[53] In-country consultations with government and industry representatives reflect that despite a number of reforms to incentivize training by employers (e.g., Law 78 on exemptions from enterprise tax; Article 3 removing value-added taxes on training courses; customs tax exemptions from the import of training materials that are unavailable in the country), there still remained a gap.

Low employer-led training rates in the country could be explained by two sources of market failures:

(i) There are information asymmetries pertaining to a limited awareness of the new skills that are required for 4IR. In-country consultations with stakeholders reveal a lack of national or industry-wide frameworks that map 4IR technologies to new skill needs.

(ii) Another area of information asymmetry is the lack of knowledge by employers and their workers about the availability of 4IR-relevant courses by training institutions. Of the training institutions, 39% surveyed highlighted a lack of knowledge about programs among trainees as a key barrier to fill courses on 4IR (Chapter 2).

Given the above, it is critical to develop a set of support programs to encourage firms to invest in relevant 4IR training for their workers. A starting point to address these incentives could be to survey employers to better understand the barriers to more investment in training, and to test a range of possible incentives. This could include options such as tax relief in exchange for employees going through training programs (whether through TVET, third-party training institutes, or in-house) or offering delivery of TVET programs on-site for large employers. The cost-benefit of each scheme would then need to be rigorously assessed before being piloted. Box 12 provides some international examples that could inform Viet Nam's approach.

This action could be potentially led by a joint committee including the Ministry of Planning and Investment (given the financial resources required to be deployed), the Ministry of Industry and Trade, the Ministry of Labor, Invalids, and Social Affairs, as well as the Ministry of Education and Training. To ensure that the schemes will be taken up by industry eventually, associations and key employers would need to be consulted during the design process.

---

53   World Economic Forum. 2018. *The Future of Jobs Report 2018*. http://www3.weforum.org/docs/WEF_Future_of_Jobs_2018.pdf.

Box 12: Incentive Schemes for Firm Training in the Region

The Government of Singapore provides firm subsidies for employee training course fees and absentee payroll salary costs, with higher incentives being awarded for courses that are government-certified.[a] For example, while subsidies for both government-certified and "approved certifiable" courses cover 90% to 95% of course fees, those for the approved certifiable courses have hourly caps. On the other hand, the subsidies for non-certifiable courses are lower at $2 per hour of training. Absentee payroll funding is also accessible and cover up to 95% of hourly basic salary. The Government of Malaysia has a similar program known as "Skills Upgrading Program", which provides grants covering 70% of training fees for small and medium-sized enterprises for technical and soft skills.[b]

[a] Skillsfuture Singapore. 2019. Funding Support for Employers. https://www.ssg.gov.sg/programmes-and-initiatives/funding/funding-for-employer-based-training.html.

[b] Microsoft and AlphaBeta. 2019. Preparing for AI: The Implications of Artificial Intelligence for Jobs and Skills in Asian Economies. https://news.microsoft.com/apac/2019/08/26/preparing-for-ai-the-implications-of-artificial-intelligence-for-jobs-and-skills-in-asian-economies/.

Source: Asian Development Bank and AlphaBeta.

Recommendation 7: Formulate new approaches and measures to strengthen inclusion and social protection in the context of Industry 4.0.

Beyond out-of-school programs that take place on a relatively ad hoc basis and at limited scale, Viet Nam has few formal skills and education programs targeted at vulnerable sectors of the population. With 4IR, new technologies have the propensity to further widen existing inequalities if workers with less access are not sufficiently reskilled. This inclusiveness is even more important given the inadequacies of education and training facilities in remote areas. This could involve tailoring programs to the needs of specified underserved groups to enhance their employability and ability to benefit from 4IR. The Ministry of Labor, Invalids and Social Affairs could analyze variations in access to critical skills by age, gender, geography, and economic background. This could then inform the development of targeted training programs, which could be developed in conjunction with other ministries (e.g., the Ministry of Education and Training, and the Ministry of Trade and Industry), the private sector, and civil society organizations such as nonprofit organizations. Possible approaches for such programs include providing access to online learning channels (e.g., the Ministry of Higher Education in Malaysia encourages and supports universities to create massive open online courses mandated to be made available to the general public),[54] developing targeted skills programs for specific underserved groups, and financial incentives for employers to train specific underserved communities (e.g., the Career-up Josei-kin program in Japan provides employers with subsidies for training individuals on nonregular contracts).[55]

---

[54] UNESCO. 2017. *Lifelong Learning in Transformation: Promising Practices in Southeast Asia.* https://unesdoc.unesco.org/ark:/48223/pf0000253603.

[55] Organisation for Economic Co-operation and Development. 2017. *Financial Incentives for Steering Education and Training, Getting Skills Right.* https://www.skillsforemployment.org/edmsp1/groups/skills/documents/skpcontent/ddrf/mtg5/~edisp/wcmstest4_189496.pdf.

Industry-specific priorities

While the above recommendations apply to both the logistics and agro-processing industries, there are a set of priorities unique to each industry that should be considered when implementing the respective policy actions. Aimed at tackling the underlying weaknesses in each industry's ability to reap the benefits from 4IR technologies, these priorities were formed based on the findings in the earlier chapters, as well as by in-country consultations with government, industry and training and education sector stakeholders.

Logistics Industry

- **Improve capacity of employers to deliver on-the-job training.** With the analysis in Chapter 2 finding that much of the 4IR skills development will likely need to take place on the job, and in-country stakeholder consultations revealing this was not taking place at sufficient levels currently, it is critical to enhance the capacity of employers to deliver such training. This means that greater emphasis will have to be placed on increasing employers' awareness of the importance and net benefits of on-the-job training (e.g., through engaging employers in the 4IR transformation roadmaps as outlined in Recommendation 1), enhancing the financial incentives for employers to do this (e.g., by implementing the incentive schemes outlined in Recommendation 6), and increasing their own capacity and adaptiveness to 4IR technologies (e.g., by developing flexible training programs for employers themselves as outlined in Recommendation 4).

- **Develop a standardized set of 4IR skills requirements and training curricula.** In-country consultations with industry stakeholders showed that, while there were current partnerships forged between logistics firms and educational and training institutions to improve the relevance of their curricula, these tended to take place on an ad-hoc basis (e.g., only some TVET centers have logistics majors), and were sporadic throughout the industry as well as in the education and training landscape. This has led to uncertainty about the standard required of workers in the industry and unevenness in training and education curriculums across institutions (which depend largely on the industry partners they worked with). As result, there has been a strong call by the industry for the government to standardize skill requirements for the industry (which can be achieved through the 4IR transformation roadmaps outlined in Recommendation 1), and to enforce them across all training programs (as in the modular skill certification programs outlined in Recommendation 5).

- **Leverage growth of local e-commerce industry to build 4IR readiness.** Despite the rapid growth of Viet Nam's e-commerce industry over recent years (a recent report found that the gross merchandise value of e-commerce services in the country grew at a staggering 81% per annum between 2015 and 2019),[56] the logistics industry, which is required to support this e-commerce growth, has been characterized by consulted industry stakeholders to be slow in its innovation and even a bottleneck to this growth.[57] Both industries also have the potential to benefit from IoT-enabled goods-tracking technology, as well as predictive analytics for supply chain management. There is thus a strong potential for strategic partnerships between companies from both industries that could boost 4IR adoption and knowhow in the logistics industry, while enhancing e-commerce delivery services. These partnerships could be instrumental to enhancing the effectiveness of the recommended actions for the logistics industry, for example, in developing 4IR skills roadmaps (Recommendation 1) and industry-led training efforts (Recommendation 2).

---

56   Google and Temasek. 2019. *e-Conomy SEA 2019*. https://www.blog.google/documents/47/SEA_Internet_Economy_Report_2019.pdf.
57   Based on consultation with the Ministry of Industry and Trade in July 2019.

Agro-processing Industry

- **Address the potentially disproportionate impact of technological disruption on females.** Both the employer survey and in-country consultations with industry representatives, government officials, and nongovernment organizations revealed that females are likely to be proportionately impacted by potential 4IR-related job displacements, given that they constitute a large share of workers in the industry. It is thus important that the training programs described in the recommendations incorporate gender-sensitive approaches (e.g., Recommendation 2 on industry-led TVET programs; Recommendation 4 on flexible skill certification programs; Recommendation 7 on formulation of new training approaches for vulnerable workers). These could include consideration of teaching pedagogies that have been demonstrated to be more effective for female learners (e.g., having female STEM role models as trainers).[58]

- **Enhance employers' knowledge of 4IR technologies.** The employer survey in Chapter 1 showed that most agro-processing firms are unaware of the different types of 4IR technologies, and their potential productivity benefits. This necessitates a strong focus on enhancing industry leaders and employers' understanding of 4IR in the first stage of any of the recommended policy actions. For example, before developing the skills framework within the sector-specific 4IR transformation roadmaps (Recommendation 1), government and industry stakeholders would have to work with technologists and align with the types of 4IR technologies applicable to the industry. For the agro-processing industry, this list has been shared in Section 1.4.1. It would also be similarly important to cultivate this understanding in downstream employee training programs.

- **Support 4IR knowledge transfer from large companies to micro, small, and medium-sized enterprises.** Viet Nam's agro-processing industry is an ecosystem consisting of large companies such as Vinamilk and TH Milk, and small and medium-sized family-owned companies. Being better resourced, these large companies are generally in a more advanced stage of 4IR adoption and training than micro, small, and medium-sized enterprises (MSMEs). A key concern reflected by government and industry representatives during in-country stakeholder consultations was that MSMEs would trail larger companies in terms of their 4IR preparedness, and lose competitiveness. There is thus a compelling push for knowledge transfer on 4IR adoption and skills development strategies from these large companies to MSMEs. These large companies can also be instrumental to supporting many of the policy recommendations outlined: from formulating the 4IR transformation roadmaps for the garment manufacturing industry (Recommendation 1) to co-creating the skill certification programs for the industry (Recommendation 4) that MSMEs can then refer to and incorporate into their own training programs. Where the required competencies overlap, there could even be scope for consolidated training programs led by these large companies for the benefit of MSMEs.

---

[58] Microsoft. 2018. *Closing the STEM Gap: Why STEM Classes and Careers Still Lack Girls and What We Can Do About It.* https://query.prod.cms.rt.microsoft.com/cms/api/am/binary/RE1UMWz.

APPENDIX
Participants Engaged During National Consultations

Together with ADB, the AlphaBeta team consulted a range of government and industry stakeholders in a series of initial consultations in July 2019, and subsequently through a workshop in October 2019. Refer to Tables A1 and A2 for the lists of consulted stakeholders in both engagements.

Table A1: List of Stakeholders Engaged in Initial Consultations in July 2019

Entity	Stakeholders Engaged
Government agencies	
Ministry of Labor, Invalids and Social Affairs – Directorate of Vocational Education and Training (DVET)	• Do Nang Khanh – Deputy Director General • Nguyễn Chí Trường – Director of Skills Department • Ma. Le Van Chuong – Deputy Director of Department Skills Development
Ministry of Industry and Trade	• Ms. Pham Ngo Thuy Ninh – Head of Human resource development and Training Division
National Institute for Vocational Training (Vocational research arm of Ministry of Labor)	• Ms. Dang Thi Huyen – Director, Research Center for Skills Development and Vocational Training Standards
Industry associations	
Viet Nam Chamber of Commerce and Industry (VCCI)	• Tran Thi Lan Anh – Deputy Secretary General, Director General of Bureau for Employers' Activities • Mai Hong Ngoc – Manager Bureau for Employers' Activities
Viet Nam Association for Vocational Education Training and Social Work (VAVET & SOW)	• Phan Chinh Thuc – Vice Chairman • Phan Sy Nghia – Vice Chairman & Chief of Office
Education and training institutes	
Hanoi College for Electronics – Mechanics	• Dao Quang Huy – Vice Rector • Nguyen Quang Huy – Head of International Relations
Research institutes	
Central Institute for Economic Management (CIEM)	• Nguyen Dinh Cung – President • Nguyen Minh Thao – Researcher

Source: Asian Development Bank and AlphaBeta.

Table A2: List of Stakeholders Engaged in Country Workshop in October 2019

Entity	Stakeholders engaged
Government agencies	
Ministry of Industry and Trade	• Duong Huong Quynh • Pham Ngo Thuy Ninh • Thuy Nguyen
Ministry of Labor, Invalids and Social Affairs (MOLISA)	• Le Thi Thao, Research Center for Skills and TVET Standards • Nguyen Chi Truong, Director, DVET • Phung Le Khanh, Director
Ministry of Planning and Investment (MPI)	• Nguyen Quynh Trang
Ministry of Education and Training	• Pham Van Son, Former Director
Industry associations	
Viet Nam Chamber of Commerce and Industry	• Pham Thi Phuong Thao
Education and training institutes	
Institute of Labour Science and Social Affairs	• Dao Quang Vinh
Viet Nam Association for Vocational Education Training and Social Work	• Phan Chinh Thuc, Vice Chairman • Phan Sy Nghia, Vice Chairman and Chief of Office
Research institutes	
Central Institute for Economic Management (CIEM)	• Ngo Minh Tuan, Deputy Director
VASS – Center for Analysis and Forecast	• Nguyen Thu Huong, Researcher
ILSSA – Research Center for Population and Labor	• Trinh Thu Nga, Director
Multilateral organizations	
International Labour Organization (ILO)	• Nguyen Thi Huyen, Project Manager
Japan International Cooperation Association (JICA)	• Pham Thi Viet Hoa, Program Officer • Sho To Mita
Deutsche Gesellschaft für Internationale Zusammenarbeit (GIZ)	• Tu, Senior Technical Advisor
Aus4Skills	• Vu Thi Binh Minh, HRD Manager

Source: Asian Development Bank and AlphaBeta.

Bibliography

Arbulu, I. et al. 2018. *Industry 4.0: Reinvigorating ASEAN Manufacturing for the Future.* McKinsey & Company. 8 February. https://www.mckinsey.com/business-functions/operations/our-insights/industry-4-0-reinvigorating-asean-manufacturing-for-the-future.

Asian Development Bank (ADB). 2014. Technical and Vocational Education and Training in the Socialist Republic of Viet Nam. Manila: ADB. https://www.adb.org/publications/technical-and-vocational-education-and-training-socialist-republic-viet-nam-assessment (accessed 7 July 2020).

ADB. 2018. Asian Development Outlook 2018 - How Technology Affects Jobs. Manila: ADB. https://www.adb.org/publications/asian-development-outlook-2018-how-technology-affects-jobs (accessed 7 July 2020).

Asia Philanthropy Circle. 2017. Catalysing Productive Livelihood: A Guide to Education Interventions with an Accelerated Path to Scale and Impact. https://www.edumap-indonesia.asiaphilanthropycircle. org/ (accessed 7 July 2020).

Association of Southeast Asian Nations (ASEAN) Secretariat. 2018. ASEAN Key Figures 2018. https://www.aseanstats.org/wp-content/uploads/2018/12/ASEAN-Key-Figures-2018.pdf (accessed 7 July 2020).

Australian Aid (AusAid), Viet Nam Logistics Research and Development Institute (VLI), and Viet Nam Logistics Business Association (VLA). 2019. Brief Report on the Current Status of the Logistics Workforce in Viet Nam. Sourced from AusAID.

Barber, M. 2008. *Instruction to Deliver: Fighting to Transform Britain's Public Services.* London: Methuen Pub. Ltd.

Bashi, Z. et al. 2019. Alternative Proteins: The Race for Market Share Is On. *McKinsey & Company.* 16 August. https://www.mckinsey.com/industries/agriculture/our-insights/alternative-proteins-the-race-for-market-share-is-on.

Behavioural Insights Team, Cabinet Office and Nesta. 2015. Easy, Attractive, Timely, Social: Four Simple Ways to Apply Behavioural Insights. https://www.behaviouralinsights.co.uk/wp-content/uploads/2015/07/BIT-Publication-EAST_FA_WEB.pdf (accessed 7 July 2020).

Boston Consulting Group. 2015. Industry 4.0: The Future of Productivity and Growth in Manufacturing Industries. https://www.bcg.com/publications/2015/engineered_products_project_business_industry_4_future_productivity_growth_manufacturing_industries (accessed 7 July 2020).

Center for Universal Education at Brookings Institution. 2019. Learning to Leapfrog: Innovative Pedagogies to Transform Education. https://www.brookings.edu/wp-content/uploads/2019/09/Learning-to-Leapfrog-InnovativePedagogiestoTransformEducation-Web.pdf (accessed 7 July 2020).

Daly, E. and S. Singham. 2012. Delivery 2.0: The New Challenge for Governments. *McKinsey & Company*. https://www.mckinsey.com/industries/public-sector/our-insights/delivery-20-the-new-challenge-for-governments (accessed 7 July 2020).

Dang, V. L. and G. T. Yeo. 2018. Weighing the Key Factors to Improve Viet Nam's Logistics System. *The Asian Journal of Shipping and Logistics*. https://www.sciencedirect.com/science/article/pii/S2092521218300774 (accessed 7 July 2020).

DHL. 2016. Robotics in Logistics. https://www.dhl.com/content/dam/downloads/g0/about_us/logistics_insights/dhl_trendreport_robotics.pdf (accessed 7 July 2020).

Dione, O. 2018. 4IR – Harnessing Disruption for Viet Nam's Development. World Bank: Speeches & Transcripts. https://www.worldbank.org/en/news/speech/2018/07/13/industry-4-harnessing-disruption-for-vietnams-development (accessed 7 July 2020).

Food and Agriculture Organization of the United Nations (FAO). 2019. State of Food and Agriculture 2019. Moving Forward on Food Loss and Waste Reduction. http://www.fao.org/3/ca6030en/ca6030en.pdf (accessed 12 August 2020).

Food Innovation Australia Limited. 2017. Food and Agribusiness: Size of the Prize Analysis for Australia. https://fial.com.au/size-of-the-prize-report (accessed 12 August 2020).

Generation Program. 2019. https://www.generation.org/ (accessed 7 July 2020).

Google and Temasek. 2019. e-Conomy SEA 2019. https://www.blog.google/documents/47/SEA_Internet_Economy_Report_2019.pdf (accessed 7 July 2020).

Government of Malaysia, Department of Skills Department. Malaysian Skill Certificate (SKM). 2017. https://www.dsd.gov.my/jpkv4/index.php/en/malaysian-skills-certificate (accessed 7 July 2020).

Government of Malaysia, Ministry of Higher Education and Malaysian Qualifications Agency. 2011. Malaysian Qualifications Framework. https://www.mqa.gov.my/pv4/mqf.cfm (accessed 12 August 2020).

Government of New Zealand, Ministry of Business, Innovation and Employment. 2019. Occupation Outlook. http://occupationoutlook.mbie.govt.nz/ (accessed 7 July 2020).

Government of Singapore, Ministry of Education. 2016. Formation of the Council for Skills, Innovation and Productivity. Press release. https://www.moe.gov.sg/news/press-releases/formation-of-the-council-for-skills--innovation-and-productivity (accessed 7 July 2020).

Government of Singapore, Ministry of Trade and Industry. 2017. Media Factsheet- Industry Transformation Maps. https://www.mti.gov.sg/-/media/MTI/ITM/General/Fact-sheet-on-Industry-Transformation-Maps---revised-as-of-31-Mar-17.pdf (accessed 7 July 2020).

Government of Viet Nam, Directorate of Vocational Education and Training (DVET). 2018. Manpower Training for Industrial Revolution 4.0. http://gdnn.gov.vn/AIAdmin/News/View/tabid/66/newsid/36805/seo/Dao-tao-nhan-luc-cho-cach-mang-cong-nghiep-4-0/Default.aspx (accessed 7 July 2020).

Government of Viet Nam, General Statistics Office. 2017. Statistical Yearbook of Viet Nam. https://web.archive.org/web/20190313120427/http://www.gso.gov.vn/default_en.aspx?tabid=515&idmid=5&ItemID=18941 (accessed 12 August 2020).

Government of Viet Nam, Ministry of Industry and Trade and United Nations Development Programme (UNDP). 2019. 4IR Readiness of Industry Enterprises in Viet Nam. https://www.vn.undp.org/content/vietnam/en/home/library/I40.html (accessed 12 August 2020).

Hasnan, N. Z. N. and Y. Yusoff. 2018. Application Areas of 4IR: Technologies in Food Processing Sector. Conference paper. https://www.semanticscholar.org/paper/Short-review%3A-Application-Areas-of-Industry-4.0-in-Hasnan-Yusoff/702d5dab564c1d32f012642dc4ce3dc0955a5b50 (accessed 7 July 2020).

Honeywell Case Studies. 2010. YCH Group Selects Intermec Fixed Vehicle Computer to Improve Supply Chain Management. https://www.varinsights.com/doc/ych-group-selects-intermec-fixed-vehicle-0003 (accessed 7 July 2020).

International Labour Organization (ILO). 2020. https://www.ilo.org/global/lang--en/index.htm (accessed 12 August 2020).

JP Morgan Chase & Co. 2019. https://www.jpmorganchase.com/corporate/Corporate-Responsibility/new-skills-stories.htm (accessed 7 July 2020).

KellyOCG. 2018. From Workforce to Workfit. https://www.kellyocg.com/insights/featured-content/whitepapers/from-workforce-to-workfit/.

Ketelhut, D. J., et al. 2009. A Multi-User Virtual Environment for Building and Assessing Higher Order Inquiry Skills in Science. *British Journal of Educational Technology*. https://onlinelibrary.wiley.com/doi/abs/10.1111/j.1467-8535.2009.01036.x (accessed 7 July 2020).

Kuczera, M. 2010. *Learning for Jobs - The OECD International Survey of VET Systems: First Results and Technical Report*. https://www.oecd.org/education/skills-beyond-school/47334855.pdf (accessed 7 July 2020).

Masters, K. 2017. *The Impact of Industry 4.0 on the Automotive Industry*. https://blog.flexis.com/the-impact-of-industry-4.0-on-the-automotive-industry (accessed 12 August 2020).

Microsoft. 2018. Closing the STEM Gap: Why Stem Classes and Careers Still Lack Girls and What We Can Do About It. https://query.prod.cms.rt.microsoft.com/cms/api/am/binary/RE1UMWz (accessed 7 July 2020).

Microsoft. 2018. The Future Computed. https://blogs.microsoft.com/wp-content/uploads/2018/02/The-Future-Computed_2.8.18.pdf (accessed 7 July 2020).

Microsoft. 2019. The Enabling Boat Connects Youth in Coastal Viet Nam. https://www.microsoft.com/inculture/enabling-boat-connects-youth-coastal-vietnam/ (accessed 12 August 2020).

Microsoft. 2019. When Dreams Become (Augmented) Reality: Preserving Australia's Indigenous Cultures. https://news.microsoft.com/life/indigenous-cultures/ (accessed 7 July 2020).

Microsoft and AlphaBeta. 2019. Preparing for AI: The Implications of Artificial Intelligence for Jobs and Skills in Asian Economies. https://news.microsoft.com/apac/2019/08/26/preparing-for-ai-the-implications-of-artificial-intelligence-for-jobs-and-skills-in-asian-economies/ (accessed 7 July 2020).

Mokhtar, F. 2018. SkillsFuture Singapore to Deepen Skills of Training and Adult Education Providers. *Today*. https://www.todayonline.com/singapore/skillsfuture-singapore-deepen-skills-training-and-adult-education-providers (accessed 7 July 2020).

Organisation for Economic Co-operation and Development (OECD). 2012. Skills Development Pathways in Asia. https://www.oecd.org/cfe/leed/Skills%20Development%20Pathways%20in%20Asia_FINAL%20VERSION.pdf (accessed 7 July 2020).

onebillion. 2020. Onecourse: One App That Delivers Reading, Writing And Numeracy. https://onebillion.org/onecourse/app/ (accessed 7 July 2020).

Oxford Economics. 2018. Technology and the Future of ASEAN Jobs. https://www.oxfordeconomics.com/recent-releases/dd577680-7297-4677-aa8f-450da197e132 (accessed 7 July 2020).

Oxford Internet Institute. 2019. Online Labour Index. https://ilabour.oii.ox.ac.uk/online-labour-index/ (accessed 7 July 2020).

Pathways for Prosperity Commission. 2019. Positive Disruption: Health and Education in the Digital Age. https://pathwayscommission.bsg.ox.ac.uk/positive-disruption (accessed 7 July 2020).

Prospera and AlphaBeta Advisors. 2019. Capturing Indonesia's Automation Potential. https://www.alphabeta.com/wp-content/uploads/2019/08/capturing-indonesias-automation-potential.pdf (accessed 7 July 2020).

PwC. 2018. The Macroeconomic Impact of Artificial Intelligence. https://www.pwc.co.uk/economic-services/assets/macroeconomic-impact-of-ai-technical-report-feb-18.pdf (accessed 7 July 2020).

Reif, R. and W. Günthner. 2009. Pick-by-vision: Augmented Reality Supported Order Picking. The Visual Computer. https://www.researchgate.net/publication/220068297_Pick-by-vision_augmented_reality_supported_order_picking (accessed 7 July 2020).

Revfine. 2018. *4 Ways Facial Recognition Can Be Used in the Travel Industry*. https://www.revfine.com/facial-recognition-travel-industry/ (accessed 7 July 2020).

Revfine. 2018. *How Artificial Intelligence is Changing the Travel Industry*. https://www.revfine.com/artificial-intelligence-travel-industry/ (accessed 7 July 2020).

Revfine. 2018. *How Blockchain Technology is Transforming the Travel Industry*. https://www.revfine.com/blockchain-technology-travel-industry/ (accessed 7 July 2020).

Revfine. 2018. *How the Internet of Things (IoT) Can Benefit the Travel Industry*. https://www.revfine.com/internet-of-things-travel-industry/ (accessed 7 July 2020).

Robotics Business Review. 2019. Reports Indicate Strong Growth Ahead for Logistics. https://www.roboticsbusinessreview.com/supply-chain/reports-indicate-strong-growth-ahead-for-logistics/ (accessed 7 July 2020).

Robotics Industry Association. 2019. Robotics in Food Manufacturing and Food Processing. https://www.robotics.org/blog-article.cfm/Robotics-in-Food-Manufacturing-and-Food-Processing/154 (accessed 7 July 2020).

Schwab, K. 2017. The Fourth Industrial Revolution. https://books.google.com.sg/books?hl=en&lr=&id=ST_FDAAAQBAJ&oi=fnd&pg=PR7&dq=klaus+schwab+fourth+industrial+revolution&ots=DTnvbTqvTQ&sig=aOLqcUCFsLKbNpjWa5kr2Sjzhu4#v=onepage&q=klaus%20schwab%20fourth%20industrial%20revolution&f=false (accessed 7 July 2020).

SkillsFuture Singapore. 2019. Funding Support for Employers. https://www.ssg.gov.sg/programmes-and-initiatives/funding/funding-for-employer-based-training.html (accessed 7 July 2020).

SkillsFuture Singapore. 2019. Skills Framework. https://www.skillsfuture.sg/skills-framework (accessed 7 July 2020).

Spector, J. M. and S. Ma. 2019. Inquiry and Critical Thinking Skills for the Next Generation: From Artificial Intelligence Back to Human Intelligence. *Smart Learning Environments*. https://slejournal.springeropen.com/articles/10.1186/s40561-019-0088-z (accessed 7 July 2020).

Tang, S. K. 2019. Singapore Businesses Not Investing Enough In Employee Training: SBF survey, Channel News Asia. https://www.channelnewsasia.com/news/business/singapore-companies-not-investing-employee-training-sbf-survey-11134230 (accessed 7 July 2020).

United Nations Educational, Scientific and Cultural Organization (UNESCO). 2017. Towards Quality Assurance of Technical and Vocational Education and Training. https://unesdoc.unesco.org/ark:/48223/pf0000259282 (accessed 7 July 2020).

UNESCO Institute for Lifelong Learning. 2017. Lifelong Learning in Transformation: Promising Practices in Southeast Asia. https://unesdoc.unesco.org/ark:/48223/pf0000253603 (accessed 7 July 2020).

Vietnamese-German Programme Reform of TVET in Viet Nam (TVET-Viet Nam). 2018. Industry boards/ Skills councils - A Mechanism Enhancing the Cooperation with the Business Sector in TVET. https://www.tvet-Viet Nam.org/en/article/1569.industry-boards-skills-councils-a-mechanism-enhancing-the-cooperation-with-the-business-sector-in-tvet.html (accessed 7 July 2020).

Woetzl, J. et al. 2014. Southeast Asia at the Crossroads: Three Paths to Prosperity. McKinsey Global Institute. November. https://www.mckinsey.com/~/media/McKinsey/Featured%20Insights/Asia%20 Pacific/Three%20paths%20to%20sustained%20economic%20growth%20in%20Southeast%20Asia/ MGI%20SE%20Asia_Executive%20summary_November%202014.ashx.

World Bank. 2014. Efficient Logistics: A Key to Viet Nam's Competitiveness, https://documents. worldbank.org/en/publication/documents-reports/documentdetail/646871468132885170/efficient-logistics-a-key-to-vietnams-competitiveness (accessed 12 August 2020).

World Bank. 2018. Viet Nam's Future Jobs: Leveraging Mega-Trends for Greater Prosperity. https://www.worldbank.org/en/country/vietnam/publication/vietnam-future-jobs-leveraging-mega-trends-for-greater-prosperity (accessed 7 July 2020).

World Bank. 2019. Viet Nam: Assessment of Logistics Skills, Training, and Competencies of Male and Female Employees. Sourced from World Bank.

World Bank Group and LinkedIn Corporation. 2020. Digital Data for Development, licensed under CC BY 3.0. https://linkedindata.worldbank.org/ (accessed 7 July 2020).

World Economic Forum. 2018. The Future of Jobs Report 2018. http://www3.weforum.org/docs/WEF_ Future_of_Jobs_2018.pdf (accessed 7 July 2020).

www.ingramcontent.com/pod-product-compliance
Lightning Source LLC
Chambersburg PA
CBHW050049220326
41599CB00045B/7337